THE TRAVELING

IEP

The Individualized Education Plan
and How It Can Be Successful by
Traveling to College

Toby Tomlinson Baker, Ph.D.

The Traveling IEP: The Individualized Education Plan and
How It Can Be Successful by Traveling to College

Copyright @ 2023 by Toby Tomlinson Baker, Ph.D.

All rights reserved in all media. No part of this book may be used or reproduced without written permission, except in the case of brief questions embodied in critical articles and reviews.

The moral right of Toby Tomlinson Baker,Ph.d. as the author of this work has been asserted by her in accordance with the Copyright, Designs, and Patents Act of 1988.

Published in the United States by BCG Publishing, 2023.

www.BCGPublishing.com

Table Of Contents

Introduction: What Is an IEP? 1

Chapter One: Enrollment and Departure of Postsecondary
Students with Disabilities 13

    Rehabilitation Act... 15
    Americans With Disabilities Act 17
    Departure of Postsecondary Students with Disabilities 18

Chapter Two: Specially Designed Majors 21

    Dream of Graduating 22
    Specially Designed Instruction 23

Chapter Three: Legislation That Protects College SWDs 29

    IDEA 30
    ADA.. 31

Chapter Four: Mandated Accommodations and
Academic Adjustments 35

    High School Accommodations.. 35
    College Academic Adjustments 36
    The Vanishing IEP 38
    504 Plans... 39
    Academic Adjustments 40

Chapter Five: Concealing Your Disability 44

    Adaptive Coping Strategies 45
    Read Your IEPs! 46

Chapter Six: What Students Think Professors Believe 51

    Combatting the Stigma.. 52
    What Professors Think of SWDs 53

Chapter Seven: Faculty Perceptions 59

Expectations and Misconceptions 60
I'm a professor, not a teacher 61
What do faculty really know about disabilities? 65

Chapter Eight: The Value of Mentorship 73

Chapter Nine: Tailored Disability Training for College Faculty 78

Faculty and Institutions' Reservations 79
Tailored Disability Training 81
Current Policies and Procedures 82

Chapter Ten: The Traveling IEP 85

Section 504 and the HEOA 85
Introducing the RISE Act 87
Faculty's Hesitation for The Traveling IEP 91
OSA 92
The Vision of the Traveling IEP 94
Actionable Steps 96
Conclusion 98

Chapter Eleven: Graduate Students with Disabilities 99

Resources 103

References 108

Appendices 120

About the Author 126

Notes 128

List of Tables

Table 1: U.S. Legislators and Status of Bills That Promote the
IEP in Higher Education 90

List of Figures

Figure 1: Framework Guiding Faculty's Knowledge, Compliance, and Perceptions 27

Figure 2: U.S. Special Education Legislation Framework 32

Figure 3: Best Practices and Mandated Accommodations for K-12 Students With Disabilities and Academic Adjustments for Postsecondary Students with Disabilities. 37

Figure 4: Adaptive Coping Strategies for Postsecondary Students with Disabilities 45

Figure 5: High School Versus College Framework 49

Figure 6: Example Statements by Faculty 56

Figure 7: Article Published in PennLive 89

Figure 8: Box of the Traveling IEP Accommodations 97

INTRODUCTION
What Is an IEP?

Most kids attend one elementary school, middle school, and high school in the same school district near their residence, with the same students, during K-12th grade. During my educational career, I have attended six different schools between kindergarten and twelfth grade. Every two years, I transferred schools. Why? Because teachers could not teach me. I was distracted, distractable, I took a long time to finish assignments and tasks, I did not listen the first time, I needed directions repeated, and I was always the last one, the kid at the end of the line.

I have a learning disability and attention deficit hyperactivity disorder, or ADHD. I looked like a typical girl with blond pigtails, but I was not. At the beginning of second grade, Mrs. Brown, an older teacher who looked like she was ready for retirement, assigned a summer writing reflection to the class. I loved writing! This would be easy for me. I was sitting in the first seat of the front row as the class began writing. I couldn't remember if Mrs.

Brown provided a writing model on the board with her expectation, but I remember writing on lined paper, a full page, single-spaced and back-to-back, about our visit to Ocean City, New Jersey. I wrote in detail, describing the shells I found on walks with my dad, watching the sunset from the wooden deck, eating fudge from the boardwalk, and the Tilt-A-Whirl ride. And many other wonderful things about that trip to the shore. This was my writing masterpiece, and I couldn't wait to share it with everyone!

I was busy writing and I heard, "Why is Toby still writing?"

I looked up and all the other students had finished the assignment. Mrs. Brown walked over to my desk and snatched my page from under me.

"You didn't follow directions," she said. "You must do your writing this way."

I couldn't believe what happened next. Mrs. Brown frowned and crumpled my paper into a ball in her fist and said I would have to redo the assignment. She directed me to look at another student's work for the model, so I looked at Jean's paper that only had three lousy sentences! I was appalled. I had written so much more and with much better description. I believed what I'd written was far superior as far as writing assignments went. I had written much more than simply three measly sentences.

Mrs. Brown made me feel unworthy as a writer, so much so, that as an adult I remember her reaction to my writing. She had me redo the assignment and sent a note to my parents. Later, I realized that it wasn't about my writing, but that I had not followed her directions and, therefore, I was unable to focus on classroom tasks. Mrs. Brown had a rigid way of teaching and demanded assignments be completed to her satisfaction. She was the teacher. Not the way I wanted to complete the assignment—the way she wanted it completed. This was the first time I realized I was not in control or involved in my education.

Prior to being diagnosed with a learning disability (and ADHD) my perspective, as a child, was not centered on having a disability, but rather why the adults were not being fair to me at school. Difficulties completing my assignments occurred all year with Mrs. Brown. I took too long to read our comprehension stories, I could not remember what I had just read, and I rarely finished my assignments as fast as the other students. I could not remember any of my teacher's lectures about the content. Moreover, I struggled to retain any math concepts, so consequently, I missed a lot of recess that year, and I really needed to have a recess break. On my report card, my teacher wrote that I was distractable but persevered when tasks were difficult. Plainly put, I probably was not listening and was daydreaming, but when I was redirected, I tried hard to learn. I wanted to please my teachers and my parents.

Sometime in June, my parents told me that I was not successful at this school and would go to third grade at a different school a little farther away. Why did I have to change schools?

The new school had something called a Resource Room. Without quite knowing what was going on, I had been diagnosed with a specific learning disability and dyscalculia that year in Mrs. Brown's class.

What was missing though, was that during the 1980s, brave, talkative little blond girls like me, who frequently interrupted their teachers and twirled their hair when they were bored, often went undiagnosed with attention deficit hyperactivity disorder, better known as ADHD. I went all through K-12 school and college before I received my first diagnosis of ADHD.

During college, it seemed to me that I had to convince my professors that I was intelligent. They probably looked at me and thought I was a little kid since I am petite. During high school, I had not been strong in math and science, yet I excelled in reading and writing. I earned a 99% on my senior English midterm exam, and I learned every definition in my government and economics class. I *am* smart and creative. During high school, I received accommodations at the Resource Room. Some of my high school teachers were shocked that I was admitted into college. Why, when I began in college, did I have to prove my academic ability to my professors?

Later in my life, upon earning my Ph.D., I began teaching as an adjunct professor the following fall after graduation. As I accomplished each of my goals, I thought of all the people who told me I would never graduate from college or become a credentialed teacher. Why had they doubted my ability to achieve success in an academic field? I had not only become an award-winning teacher, but I became a college professor of curriculum and education credentialing. I imagined that they could see me now, despite their suspicions of my degrees, and I wish I could say to them, "Not bad for a girl with a learning disability and ADHD."

I had never really thought of myself as an academic or scholar, creating syllabi and lecturing a few evenings a week, but here I am, doing it. As a teacher, I have written many IEPs for students throughout the years and honed my skills in IEP compliance. More importantly though, I see the student and person behind the IEP paperwork since I have been there.

More importantly though, I see the student and person behind the IEP paperwork since I have been there. I know what it was like to have a psychologist explain why I was not good at "school." When I was fourteen years old, I sat in a psychologist's office as she explained in detail what aspects of the assessment were my strengths and where my areas of need were. At fourteen years old, it was hard to hear how far behind I was academically from the other students. The psychologist told my parents that I was well below basic in math. Yet I did not feel as if I was behind everyone else. I did not agree with these strangers' reports. How did they really know what to write in their reports since they did not know me? What would I want my evaluators and teachers to write in my IEP? As a result of this meeting, I became very interested in my education and vocal about choice of schools.

First, what is an IEP? An IEP is an acronym for an Individualized Education Plan and, simply stated, is an education plan that is mandated by the federal law to serve students with disabilities in K-12 settings. The Individuals with Disabilities Education Act (IDEA)[1] outlines everything that educators and district service providers must do to serve a student with a disability (Appendix I, Definitions of Special Education Terms and Acronyms). An IEP also specifically details *how* the education will be served to the student. This is where an IEP gets technical. Do parents really know exactly how many minutes (not hours) a week their child receives which service? Unfortunately, this is where most parents and teachers get lost.

Many people know the term IEP because it is used so extensively throughout K-12 education, but for those who are not familiar, it is the Individualized Educational Plan for a student with a diagnosis of a disability. It is consulted and followed by the student's teachers and administrators who serve this student. There should be copies of the student's previous IEPs stored in their cumulative folders. The IEP is the actionable response to the national disability policy, and its basis is PL 94-142, IDEA.[2]

An IEP provides services to all students who have been properly diagnosed with a disability and have been found eligible for special education services. An IEP is a written plan that specifies the individual educational needs of the student and what related services are necessary to meet the student's unique instructional needs. This means that every child receives their own IEP. That's a lot of paperwork, specifically a draft of the IEP, but special education teachers and school administrators know the system and how to make it work for individual students with disabilities (SWDs).

What are the parts of the IEP?[3]

An initial IEP is the child's very first IEP. The initial IEP can only be completed after the child has had a full comprehensive evaluation by a licensed psychologist. A teacher or principal cannot whip up an IEP for any child of their choosing. Every student who is eligible for services under an IEP has been evaluated by a psychologist.

Once a student has been determined eligible for special education services, the IEP team sets a date to meet. The IEP team could be large or small, but must always have a parent, Special Education teacher, General Education teacher, a district administrator or designee, and always a psychologist present at the initial IEP. The psychologist must be there to interpret the results of their tests and to determine the child's diagnosis. Until there is a diagnosis and confirmed eligibility, there cannot be services for the child.

Once the diagnosis has been presented and eligibility confirmed, the administrator or academic teacher can present any other parent statements, data, grades from previous schools to show where the child/student is performing *presently*, meaning currently. In the special education world these are called Present Levels of Performance, or abbreviated, PLPs or PLOPs, or PLEPs, depending on your district or state. PLOPs are where your child/student is performing academically (or behaviorally) now. It follows that the IEP's Annual Goals are added after the PLPs, therefore signifying the future—what the child/student would have accomplished in one year. Goals are written in such a way that they are measurable and attainable. If these aspects are not agreed upon during the meeting, they can be rewritten at a parent's request. These goals should reflect the PLPs and the specific area of need.

How is the child/student going to meet these goals? Through accommodations and modifications outlined in Free Appropriate Public Education (FAPE), which specifically itemizes each service, down to the exact minutes. Finally, when a student turns fifteen years old, they should be offered a strategic transition plan. Parents should familiarize themselves with this and ask if their child's high school has a counselor or transition specialist. Many high schools do not, so parents have the option to pursue assistance with transitions by contacting the school district or local education agency.

Beyond this there are testing accommodations, Designated Instructions Services (DIS), and compensatory services that need to be explained and addressed with the parents. If the parent agrees, they will sign the district IEP agreement. And the IEP becomes active. I have seen IEPs that take a week to develop and implement and others that take years. Certain aspects may vary depending on your state and school district; however, these are the critical parts of an IEP. Keep in mind, IEPs are strictly limited to K-12 school-aged students.

What is missing in higher education or college settings is the requirement for IEPs to be utilized and to implement those which students with disabilities are accustomed to receiving. What's more, SWDs may not realize that their college or other postsecondary settings will not be using IEPs.

A few years ago, I conducted a case study and interviewed higher education faculty and asked them if they thought there should be IEPs utilized in college. Yes! I uncovered what higher education faculty knew about IEPs and accommodations and found they were not well-versed in disability law. My faculty participants stated more training was needed to provide accommodations to postsecondary students with disabilities.

What *does* special education look like for each student according to their IEP? It may include accommodations such as a smaller setting with six to ten students to minimize distractions during academic instruction. Maybe smaller instruction is needed only during test taking. Special education services could mean that a student receives speech therapy two or three times weekly. It could mean that the student receives support from a school counselor or that they may use assistive technology to access their program. It may mean that the student receives one-on-one assistance from a trained aide during each hour of their school day. All these services are discussed and amended during a team meeting with parents, teachers, administrators, and psychologists who determine what services are needed for the student's academic success. Often, educational law is needed to guide these decisions.

There are many supports or accommodations, changes that allow a person with a disability to participate fully in an activity or K-12 school program. An *accommodation* written and stated in a student's IEP changes how a student will be taught the state-mandated (not optional) K-12 academic curriculum and allows for equal access to education. Additionally, IEPs must be reviewed annually by a team, including the child's current K-12 teacher, a K-12 school administrator, and the parent. And finally, IEPs are utilized in K-12 settings only, throughout the nation for all eligible SWDs.

But the IEP does not travel to college.

Imagine this: a country where all SWDs can graduate from high school, enroll and attend college, and keep their IEP services and accommodations throughout their college years. Many SWDs successfully graduated from high school and entered college, and they had IEPs or learning plans that are comparable with Specially Designed Instruction. Why not continue to have these services and accommodations during college?

The question I address throughout this book is:

What supports were written in the student's IEP and provided to that student during K-12th grades that supported the student toward graduation?

And *why* don't IEPs (along with those supports and accommodations) travel to college?

Why don't colleges and universities honor and employ the IDEA legislation? What would IEPs at every college nationwide look like? Many skeptics have asked me this question, and I challenge them. Why *not* have the Traveling IEP? This book provides answers for these skeptics and offers a solid plan for moving forward with the Traveling IEP in higher education.

My vision is for every postsecondary student with a documented disability who received services with an IEP during elementary and secondary school to receive the same accommodations and services in college. Aside from the obvious, the paperwork, the thick thirty- to forty-page document detailing the minutes of a particular service, is the greater issue. The educators. I aim to make college faculty knowledgeable... knowledgeable in understanding IEPs. I know that IEPs are a life-changing document for a student with a disability. It should not stop simply because high school ended.

If you have read this far, you have been introduced to the term IEP; however, the word traveling may be a new concept. I am championing this idea of the Traveling IEP because at the present time, there is no provision for an IEP that was utilized during high school to travel to college with a student who has a disability. That simple concept is the basis for this book, both as a policy proposal and because of my personal story. It is my firm belief that the Traveling IEP will remedy many issues of those hundreds of thousands of students entering postsecondary education!

CHAPTER ONE

Enrollment and Departure of Postsecondary Students with Disabilities

As a child during the 1980s, I was diagnosed with a learning disability (LD), and I believe that if I had been born ten years earlier, I probably would not have gone to college. The laws that protected people with disabilities were still ideas, not written as public law. Who knows if I would have a job: a good job with benefits and high pay? During mid-1970s when the Rehabilitation Act[4] was passed and IDEA[5] was enacted, students gained greater access to school buildings and public learning programs. On the surface, these disability laws amended everything that was derogatory for students who received special education services. However, the practical implementation of these laws was sporadic and unreliable.

During first grade, I was a slow reader who struggled processing what I read, and I was easily distracted. During directed reading time in second grade, I found that I always had to reread what I had read, and I noticed that my peers finished reading the section first. Then teachers asked me questions about the text and since I had not finished reading the text, I had no idea how to respond.

I was that student who teachers did not want in their class. I loved to talk about everything except the teacher's lesson content. It is not surprising to me that when I was forty years old, I was diagnosed with attention deficit hyperactivity disorder (ADHD).[6] I had gone all through school not knowing why I was distracted. I worked my butt off and studied during high school, stayed after school, and went to tutoring classes to make sure I did not fall behind. During tenth and eleventh grades, I took summer school classes in math and science to keep up with my grade-level peers. When I graduated from high school, I was surprised, but not really. I was a "Resource Room" kid. I had gotten one-to-one assistance from the Resource Room during high school and the extra support that allowed me to achieve. I graduated from high school in June with the intent on entering college in the fall.

I was accepted to Moravian College, yet the institution attached conditions, which I found to be very sneaky. The deans were being cautious; I had to prove that I could succeed as a college student, so they wrote a letter to me stating that I could start in the fall if I passed two courses at a local college. I immediately took two government courses at West Chester

University during the summer. One of the professors suggested that college was not for me, but of course, I was going to college! I was appalled that he suggested that I *not* go to college. I did pass both courses, and, therefore, I was admitted to college in the fall.

Rehabilitation Act

As a freshman, I think I was so afraid of failing that I was hyperfocused: obsessive-compulsive about passing my classes. I remember thinking I was the only student with a disability at the entire college, which probably was not true, but it seemed true. Students with disabilities understandably did not self-disclose. But I did not know anyone else like me at Moravian. There was no "Resource Room" in college.

In the past, many high school graduates with disabilities were absent from college. They may have been detained, institutionalized, or discouraged from attending college. Until the two major disability laws, the Rehabilitation Act and IDEA, emerged, SWDs like me were not expected to attend college like their grade-level peers.[7] Even if they were allowed to graduate with a valid high school diploma, what would they do? Go to college? Why? SWDs were not academics or scholars; therefore, they did not attend college. I was an exception, and I didn't like being the exception.

Although the Rehabilitation Act of 1973 promoted greater access to colleges for SWDs, it primarily addressed the concerns of national infrastructure more than practical academic accommodations. For instance, students who used wheelchairs had previously been denied access to universities because university buildings did not have accessible ramps, sidewalks, or elevators. The Rehabilitation Act changed this obstacle and addressed the need for funding for these changes.[8]

Unfortunately, even though the Rehabilitation Act caused a national upheaval for equal access for people with disabilities, it did not bring about much social change specifically for in-class support for postsecondary students who required academic accommodations. This act did not promote improved academic support provided to all students with disabilities. There were still limited disability services on college campuses. No academic support team, no Resource Room or small group instruction to supplement every professor's lectures. Notetakers were unheard of.

Until the mid-1970s, with the passing of the IDEA in 1975, many high school graduates with learning disabilities conceded and withdrew from academic society. At that time in disability history, there was minimal activism by SWDs seeking access to colleges. It seemed to be understood that they did not go there. Students with disabilities accepted that they were not college material.

Pursuing a college degree was sometimes even discouraged for nondisabled students, who may have been pushed toward employment in technical and service-oriented positions. Many students believed that they were not good at school as they had been told, so they changed their goals and track from academic to employment or service fields. They accepted that school and college were not for them.

Americans With Disabilities Act

During the 1980s and 1990s, students with learning differences began completing high school programs and gained disability rights, particularly with the Americans with Disabilities Act (ADA), which was proposed by President George H. W. Bush and passed by Congress in 1990.[9] Even so, high school graduates with disabilities were *still* less likely to pursue postsecondary education or live independently.

It was assumed by many people, particularly college admissions officers, that high school SWDs do not (or should not) advance to higher education and pursue higher education degrees. In fact, many high school administrators, such as guidance counselors, felt that some SWDs should be grateful that they graduated from high school and be satisfied. Aside from the rare examples of rebels with disabilities, such as Temple Grandin, Judith Heumann, and even Helen Keller, this national assumption encapsulated an entire generation of students who did not have the skills, preparation, or the resources, such as parent support and financial support, to attend college settings.

Efficacy, or achieving a desired result, and self-efficacy, believing in your own ability, are crucial for one's success during college.[10] As I was growing up, my parents told me that I would go to college and graduate. Their insistence that I was smart, capable, and worthy of earning a college degree fueled my persistence and determination to be admitted into college. During college, I did not meet any other students like me, with learning disabilities. I assumed since I did not meet anyone else who needed assistance, I was the only one. Twenty years later, many SWDs enroll and attend college, yet so many students are not graduating.

Departure of Postsecondary Students with Disabilities

In recent years, many colleges provided conventional support and manageable accommodations, such as extra time, a notetaker, copies of the professor's PowerPoint presentations, and lecture notes. However, these minimal supports are proving to be insufficient. Even after decades of education policy modifications, there are still necessary accommodations needed in college to effectively support students with a variety of learning differences.

Even with disability laws enacted, there is an excessive number of SWDs still dropping out of college settings each year. In 2020, 72% of all SWDs departed or dropped out of postsecondary academic settings (college and universities), including online and distance learning.[11] I was shocked by this statistic. Why are so many SWDs entering college and then *leaving* college?

At this time, there are approved colleges specifically for students with learning disabilities; however, the caliber of their academic quality may be questioned by families and students applying to them. For example, are LD-friendly colleges who accept a student's IEP comparable to Yale, Harvard, Stanford, Penn, and so forth? How about public state colleges, such as California State or Penn State? Why should a student with a learning disability settle their second-choice college? Students with learning differences should not settle by only applying to LD-friendly colleges. By doing this, it limits their options and, who knows, they might be admitted to their top-choice college and receive their appropriate accommodations.

Since 2010, the enrollment of postsecondary SWDs has gone up.[12] Although SWDs travel to college, the disability legislation, the IDEA, does *not* travel to college with them. There are many factors that influence a student's academic success, including socioeconomic status (SES), family supports, and personal healthcare and medicine to name a few, yet this book focuses on college faculty and their perspectives of SWDs. In the case study I conducted, I interviewed college faculty because I wanted to know what they knew about teaching SWDs. What was college faculty doing (or not doing) to support their SWDs, and how could they change their instruction to teach all students?

SWDs are dropping out or leaving college, and faculty can alter this grim statistic. As a college professor, I have had a few students each semester request an Incomplete grade because they had not completed the work, had increased absences from class, and stopped responding to emails. By providing authentic support, implementing more effective instructional techniques, and employing more creative solutions, higher education institutions across the nation can resolve this immense problem of college departure. College faculty can positively influence more SWDs to graduate.

CHAPTER TWO
Specially Designed Majors

During the early 2000s, there were a significant number of SWDs excelling in high school academic subjects, and, therefore, graduating. Even though academics may have been challenging for these students, because of the specialized support that had been mandated in their IEPs, they succeeded and graduated. Some students with learning differences continued an academic track and enrolled in college.

Moravian College is a small liberal arts college located in the Lehigh Valley. When I attended Moravian College during the mid-1990s, it seemed to me as if I were the only student enrolled with a learning disability. Enrollment statistics of postsecondary students with disabilities have improved since 1996, even with the Covid-19 pandemic. Disability legislation, specifically the ADA, has led to greater enrollment in higher education for SWDs, but it has also created an increased prevalence of dropouts among postsecondary SWDs. As SWDs continue to enroll in colleges and universities, there is a greater possibility that they will leave.

Dream of Graduating

By 2010, it became increasingly more common for students with learning differences to mirror their nondisabled peers by applying to college. There was a shift in their mindset. When interested adults asked, "What are your plans after high school?" the response from SWDs shifted from "I'm going to get a job" or "I don't know," and became "I'm going to college." The follow-up question is "What is your major?"

When any college student, regardless of disability status, applies and enrolls in college, they dream of graduating. They don't dream of dropping out or taking a semester off. They do not dream of receiving an "I" for incomplete. College students with disabilities dream of walking across the stage in their overpriced cap and gown and moving the tassel to the other side. Even when they know it will be a long and difficult journey, postsecondary SWDs dream of graduating!

As a freshman at Moravian College, I was excited that I could choose any course I wanted. I wanted to take everything. One afternoon, I was meeting with my academic advisor, Dr. McDermott, an old man who looked at me as if he would rather be anywhere than meeting with me. However, this was his job: advise the lost young student who had no idea what she wanted to do in life.

I asked him, "What if I do not ever choose a major?"

Dr. McDermott replied, "Then you won't graduate."

I realized that for me to graduate from college, I had to choose a major. That meant there would be classes I was not particularly fond of and even required classes that I would hate, but I had to graduate, so I had to take them. I had to graduate. I regret that I did not have the same structured support in college that I had had during high school. During high school, most SWDs received Specially Designed Instruction per their IEPs. Specially Designed Instruction outlines the supports students have during high school that enabled them to succeed each year up to their high school graduation. What support was *removed* when they entered college? The missing component for postsecondary SWDs is the continuation of solid disability legislation, namely, the IDEA.[13]

Per the written law, the IDEA, SWDs were supported with Specially Designed Instruction as detailed in their IEP. Specially Designed Instruction is written explicitly in the IDEA and educators are expected to execute the learning strategies recommended in this document.[14] Because SWDs in high school received Specially Designed Instruction per their IEPs, they were successful with academics because they received the academic support that they required to achieve success. Consequently, they graduated.

Specially Designed Instruction

Specially Designed Instruction is the law for SWDs during K-12 education in the United States, as it is linked through the IDEA public law.[15] Eligible students must receive Specially Designed

Instruction per their Free Appropriate Public Education in a student's IEP. The Office of Civil Rights ensures that all students have equal access to education or a Free Appropriate Public Education.

During college though, Specially Designed Instruction does not exist for postsecondary SWDs. Ideally, students' majors could mirror Specially Designed Instruction. Students would be able to choose their majors knowing that they had the exact support they needed to achieve their educational goals. Higher education administration would oversee faculty involvement to ensure that the specific support provided would lead to SWDs' success.

The crucial component of fully supporting SWDs during high school was their IEP. Students were provided individualized educational programs that included Specially Designed Instruction that had their specific academic goals. These goals were monitored consistently, with scheduled progress monitoring, during each semester until graduation. Each time an SWD's report card was issued to the parents or guardian, the student's goals were reviewed. Educators, along with IEP team members, would recommend changes or amendments to the IEP if a student was not meeting their academic goals for each semester. Each student's academic progress was analyzed for continued growth and compared to their grade-level peers. According to landmark cases such as *Timothy W. vs. Rochester*, there is a Zero Reject policy in place, which means that all students with disabilities are entitled to receive services, even if they only make minimal progress.[16]

The Local Education Agency (LEA) or school district oversees its administration to ensure compliance with these documents, particularly the assistant principal, elementary instructional specialist. Special education teachers are held accountable for implementing the support and services (the IEP) to the student. Unfortunately, many colleges and universities do not provide this level of one-on-one support to students because it is not written in the law as it is for K-12 students. Perhaps if all colleges and universities provided Specially Designed Instruction, more SWDs would graduate.

As a result of the IDEA policies, enrollment in postsecondary settings ensued.[17] Even though SWDs graduate from high school and go to college, their legislative rights through the IDEA and their rights to receive Specially Designed Instruction do *not* travel to college with them.

Upon transitioning to college, SWDs' IEPs are no longer valid or accepted by many colleges. Their IEP is discontinued or vanishes! IEPs do not physically disappear, but rather the IDEA no longer protects these students and the existing legislative coverage that they had during their K-12 school years becomes immaterial. Therefore, students do not receive Specially Designed Instruction as they had during high school.

As the IEP does not travel to college and is, therefore, not accepted paperwork for postsecondary SWDs, higher education institutions do not recognize IEPs or individual student accommodations as specified by the IDEA. How can postsecondary SWDs succeed if they have their approved accommodations completely wiped out? The consequences can be devastating for these students. The student may suffer and be at risk of dropping out or failing out of their college program.[18]

Presently, there is an increasing need for all higher education faculty to comprehend fully, articulate, and demonstrate their capacity for implementing Specially Designed Instruction. Since college professors are experts in their field, they need to learn instructional techniques that are effective with all their students. They must effectively educate their SWDs.

College professors must adapt their current instructional techniques in the higher education classroom. Many professors tend to be set in their ways. How are they going to change their instruction, their delivery, and their attitudes toward every student they teach? On a national level, professors must develop a universal solution and institutional model; professors and their institutions will have what they need to instruct postsecondary SWDs, beyond just general training.

The application of assistance, implementation, and enforcement of academic adjustments by higher education faculty is necessary for equal access to higher education for postsecondary SWDs. Figure 1 displays the conceptual framework for this book and how special education training is necessary for higher education faculty.[19] The framework shown in Figure 1 upholds that upon receiving institutional training in special education and adaptive pedagogy techniques, higher education faculty will demonstrate success in acquiring knowledge, embracing faculty compliance, and improving upon their perceptions of SWDs. Most important, it illustrates how the faculty's involvement impacts the student's success.[20]

Figure 1:

Framework Guiding Faculty's Knowledge, Compliance, and Perceptions

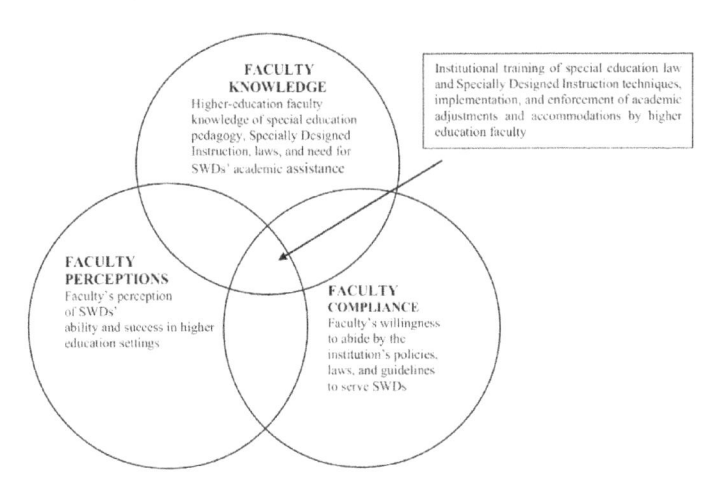

FACULTY KNOWLEDGE
Higher-education faculty knowledge of special education pedagogy, Specially Designed Instruction, laws, and need for SWDs' academic assistance

Institutional training of special education law and Specially Designed Instruction techniques, implementation, and enforcement of academic adjustments and accommodations by higher education faculty

FACULTY PERCEPTIONS
Faculty's perception of SWDs' ability and success in higher education settings

FACULTY COMPLIANCE
Faculty's willingness to abide by the institution's policies, laws, and guidelines to serve SWDs

This framework distinguishes and draws conclusions among three significant areas where higher education needs development associated with educating SWDs. These three areas are: (a) faculty knowledge of special education pedagogy, particularly in understanding Specially Designed Instruction outlined by the IDEA of 2004; (b) the perceptions that higher-education faculty have of their postsecondary SWDs; and (c) higher-education faculty's willingness to comply with national policies and laws that address the needs of postsecondary SWDs.[21]

One reason students may not be receiving their accommodations is that they are not receiving the proper accommodations from college faculty. Faculty members can change this. Great professors who obtain knowledge of special education, have a positive perception of postsecondary SWDs, and comply with university demands of accessibility, are the professors who have the highest success rate with SWDs for graduating and becoming upstanding citizens.

CHAPTER THREE

Legislation That Protects College SWDs

When SWDs enter college, it is assumed that they understand all the disability legislation that protect them. This couldn't be further from the truth. Most students, parents, and college professors have no idea what legislation protects postsecondary SWDs.

In the United States, K-12 LEAs, namely school districts, have educators and administrators who are trained to support SWDs. They must carry out the specifics that are written in each child's plan in conjunction with disability legislation, particularly the IDEA.

In the US, colleges and universities use the ADA as their official disability legislation. The ADA does not include Specially Designed Instruction as does the IDEA that had been applied during an SWD's high school experience. Consequently, because the law shifts in higher education, postsecondary SWDs are not receiving proper instructional techniques and individual accommodations.

IDEA

Even though there are a few (and I mean a few) colleges that accept former IEPs and educational evaluations, many colleges and universities in the United States do not accept IEPs or learning plans, since this paperwork is specifically tied with the IDEA, and colleges do not use this legislation. The IDEA is limited, thus, only serving SWDs during K-12.

Specially Designed Instruction as detailed in the IDEA places a heavy emphasis on one-on-one instruction between students and faculty.[22] However, the IDEA of 2004 currently does not apply to postsecondary students to ensure that they receive their needed accommodations. Even revisions developed in the IDEA Parts B and C from 2021 only focus on services for toddlers and youth.[23] Receiving Specially Designed Instruction can affect whether a postsecondary SWD graduates from college.

Federal legislation that provides support to SWDs during their K-12 education varies greatly during college. Much federal disability legislation about the transition and success in college has not been updated since the early 2000s and, therefore, transition experts rely on existing legislation to support SWDs. Disability law varies in higher education, which may lead to less academic support from professors and departure OF SWDs and departure from higher education settings. Consequently, since the disability legislative coverage has changed, so has the support.

Throughout each decade, previous legislation has been passed to protect SWDs, such as Section 504 Rehabilitation Act, the IDEA, and the Higher Education Opportunity Act (HEOA).[24] In 2015, the Every Student Succeeds Act replaced No Child Left Behind and supported strong educator accountability efforts for all students.[25] In 2008, the HEOA, Title VII, was enacted, trusting that colleges and universities would enforce and provide reasonable academic and classroom accommodations upon request to postsecondary SWDs. Yet higher education institutions are not using the HEOA as legislative coverage and still lean on the ADA.

ADA

There are certain aspects of the ADA that may be unknown to educators and administrators in higher education. When I conducted my case study and asked college professors and deans about the ADA and its supports, there were crickets-silence. Here is what I discovered through research: the ADA protects postsecondary SWDs against discrimination. The ADA does not provide funding, and neither does it address the academic resources and services of SWDs, specifically special education accommodations. The IDEA of 2004 supports only K-12 students; therefore, when a high school student with a disability does graduate from high school, their IEP becomes obsolete. If an SWD enrolls in a college or university in the United States, these higher education institutions utilize the ADA of 1990 as official disability legislation.

Figure 2:

U.S. Special Education Legislation Framework

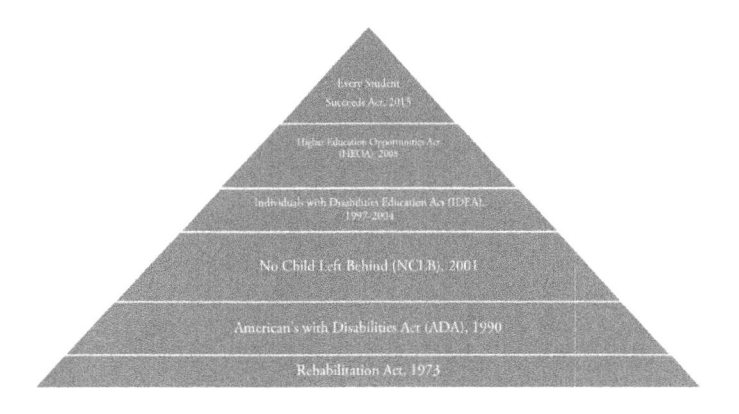

```
Every Student Succeeds Act, 2015
Higher Education Opportunities Act (HEOA), 2008
Individuals with Disabilities Education Act (IDEA), 1997-2004
No Child Left Behind (NCLB), 2001
American's with Disabilities Act (ADA), 1990
Rehabilitation Act, 1973
```

This figure illustrates the main components of each special education law.

The ADA loosely supports SWDs and does not provide specific academic accommodations to each postsecondary SWD. Furthermore, the ADA focuses on discrimination and not academic accommodations.[26] Contrary to the ADA, the IDEA does provide limited federal funding for the education of children with disabilities ages three to twenty-one, as well as expanding the protections and requires that states agree to provide a Free Appropriate Public Education that mandates Specially Designed Instruction be provided at no cost to the parents. However, the IDEA is an underfunded mandate and compliance measures of adequate funding are still being disputed.[27]

Section 504

Section 504 of the Rehabilitation Act requires schools, public or private, that receive federal financial assistance for educational purposes, not to discriminate against children with disabilities. Additionally, they must provide reasonable accommodations, yet they are not required to enforce this mandate. Comparably, higher education institutions do not have to enforce similar mandates. Currently, both Section 504 and Title II protect school-age K-12 students from discrimination, yet this legislation does not carry over or travel with the student to their higher education setting.[28]

The lack of compliance by educators with this national mandate impacts the appropriate accommodations implemented during a student's K-12 education. Consequently, the disregard of college faculty affects postsecondary SWDs who pursue degrees. For example, even though SWDs are guaranteed rights for coverage of a disability, they may not receive the same and necessary services and accommodations in higher education.[29] Bluntly stated, special education services may be neglected by K-12 educators and school districts for many reasons (lack of funding, resources, knowledge of implementation), and these services that have gone to the wayside will not magically appear once the SWD graduates from high school and goes to college. On the contrary, the student may receive even less.

Even though there has been a significant increase of postsecondary SWDs, not all colleges and universities in the United States have adapted their programs to equally serve all students. What seems to be even more challenging is the perspective university officers and higher education faculty hold regarding SWDs. Today, there is still a notion that academic scholars could not possibly be SWDs. It seems impossible that they could be one and the same. Several university officers are skeptical of accepting SWDs to their university. Higher education faculty tend to be more hesitant of instructing SWDs and question their ultimate success in college programs.

By having IEPs during college, college program designers could align the student goals with their majors. This would eliminate students taking courses they will not need and place a streamlined program toward success. It would save SWDs much time and money and would ultimately lead to their graduation.

CHAPTER FOUR

Mandated Accommodations and Academic Adjustments

Institutional officers and faculty at colleges and universities were stunned by the increasing enrollment of postsecondary SWDs during the 2010s. This upward shift is a direct reflection of improved disability legislation, especially the IDEA. In 2004, the IDEA was reauthorized and included greater transition measures for graduating high school seniors with disabilities. Even though the transition process that was written in the new IDEA legislation spelled out specific courses of action for high school graduates with disabilities, it did not include the option of having Specially Designed Instruction for each college student who had been previously provided it during high school.

High School Accommodations

During high school, SWDs tend to have a completely different experience than they do during college. Their schedules are more structured since they are bound to the daily school schedule.

Students with disabilities usually attend school during the day, with several trusted teachers, tutors, and administrators taking care of their academic progress. Moreover, these students tend to live at home where their family supports them. Since many SWDs have trusted people to assist them whenever they need help, their structured schedule, and their family to care for them 24/7, consequently, they don't develop their independence as readily as their nondisabled counterparts. Graduating seniors with disabilities have a broad safety net, and unfortunately, it is not easy to pack their safety net and bring it with them to college.

College Academic Adjustments

When SWDs start college, there may be some rude awakenings and some major adjustments (I will get to this in a moment). As far as academics and schoolwork, there are usually basic accommodations provided at colleges and universities such as extra time on assignments and tests and smaller settings to minimize distractions, but other accommodations are optional. Unless the student with a disability specifically makes a request for an accommodation, it will not be offered by the university. The student must be proactive and request exactly what they need in writing to the Office of Student Accessibility (OSA) or Disability Office (usually in the form of email or a formal letter).

Colleges and universities are not mandated or even required to provide accommodations in the same manner that K-12 schools are mandated by law. Instead, postsecondary institutions are required to *provide appropriate academic adjustments* to ensure that the institution does not discriminate based on disability.[30] Yet academic adjustments may be rejected by any professor. Figure 3 shows the stark comparison between mandated accommodations and optional academic adjustments.

Figure 3:

Best Practices and Mandated Accommodations for K-12 Students With Disabilities and Academic Adjustments for Postsecondary Students with Disabilities.

List of Best Practices and Mandated Accommodations for Pre-K-12 Students With Disabilities:

Preferential seating
Scaffolding (support)
Chunking/breaking down activities
Tasks into smaller parts
Differentiation of instruction
Small group instruction
Adapted curriculum
counseling
Extra time to complete tasks
Repetition
Graphic organizers
Drafts prior to grade
Visuals
Hands-on activities
Increased creativity
Prompting/cues/pointing
Visual cues
Modeling
Redirection
Pair activities/peer assistance
Noise buffers
Directions read aloud in a different way
Models of expectations
Specialized materials
Modified testing
Life skills development procedures
Speech to text (Read aloud)
Schedule
expectations described prior to task
Assistive technology
Deaf and Hard of Hearing Services (DHH)
(Baker, 2019)

List of Standard Academic Adjustments for Postsecondary Students With Disabilities:

Preferential seating (Student Request/Professor option)
Peer assistance/note taking (Student Request/Professor option)
Chunking/breaking down activities (Student Request/Professor option)
Differentiation of instruction (Student Request/Professor option)
Extra time to complete tasks (Student Request/Professor option)
Repetition (Student request/Professor option)
Graphic organizers (Student request/Professor option)
Drafts prior to grade (Student Request/Professor option)
Visuals (Student Request/Professor option)
Models of expectations (Student Request/Professor option)
Copies of Prof. printed Power Points (Student Request/Professor option)
expectations described prior to task (Student Request/Professor option)
Different testing room with proctor (Campus Accessibility Services)
Assistive technology (Campus Accessibility Services)
Deaf/Hard Hearing Services (DHH) (Campus Accessibility Services)
(Baker, T.T., 2020)

K-12 Best Practices/Accommodations *Missing* From Postsecondary Institutions

Scaffolding
Tasks into Smaller parts
Counseling
Increased creativity
Visual cues
Picture Exchange Communication (PECs-students with Autism)
Modeling/Redirection
Specialized Materials
Pair activities
(OT/PT/SP)
Modified testing
OTHERS BASED ON STUDENT NEED
Small group instruction
Adapted curriculum
Hands-on activities
Prompting/cues/pointing
life skills development
schedule
Speech-to-Text/Read aloud
Related Services

Here is my Yellow Sheet. On one side of the sheet is a list of best practices and mandated accommodations for Pre-K–12th grade SWDs and the comparison list of standard academic adjustments for postsecondary SWDs. The left side of this sheet contains accommodations that are written in the IDEA law and that I use and many special education teachers use when they write IEPs. The right side of this chart exemplifies how these previously mandated student accommodations are now optional, not mandated in the law. Basically, a student could request an accommodation and the professor has the option to say no. Yucky!

The Vanishing IEP

Imagine this: you have struggled all through elementary and high school because core subjects such as reading, writing, and math were challenging. Every subject had textbooks with abstract concepts and online readings, which were assigned, were difficult to understand, and not relatable. You required some accommodations such as extra time, a private setting to take tests to minimize distractions, and test directions explained to you prior to beginning an assessment.

You finally make it to your senior high school graduation. This is a joyous time. Yet a transition to college may cause more stress and doubt for graduating seniors with disabilities. Most SWDs might not be aware that their IEPs are discontinued after high school.

What does that mean? It means that even though the IDEA is solid legislation that protects K-12 SWDs, its protections are discontinued upon the student's high school graduation. That's right, the IDEA law that provided legislative support and enforced the student's mandated services, as written in their IEP, is gone! It vanishes.

The IEP doesn't truly vanish, but the student services are not protected by the law. In its place is a form titled the Summary of Performance. The Summary of Performance is part of the student's transition plan within their IEP. It is very confusing. The Summary of Performance details the student's previous accommodations that the student will employ once they have successfully transitioned to a college or university. The student will take a copy of their Summary of Performance to the College Office of Accessibility or OSA and present this document to the officer handling their file. It is the student's responsibility to share their Summary of Performance with their college or university.

In addition to transitioning to a new setting, postsecondary SWDs must make a shift between disability legislation as well. They need to know their legal rights.[31] It is particularly challenging for college freshmen to understand disability legislation and effectively articulate their academic needs to university officers. Postsecondary SWDs will not get a 504 Plan, such as the one they had during high school, and consequently, the student holds most of the responsibility.[32]

504 Plans

In the United States, SWDs are covered by national legislation in the IDEA. A student usually has a 504 Plan if they need accommodations that the school administrators and teachers can provide easily to allow a student greater access. For example, a student who utilizes a multiplication chart during class may also have a testing accommodation to use the chart during a standardized assessment. Since this student has demonstrated academic progress by using the material or device and is able to access the grade-level math curriculum by using it, the student's 504 Plan is effective. This student could be a general education student and nondisabled, yet they can benefit from accommodations.

If a student with a disability attends a state public school, they will be evaluated by a licensed psychologist paid for and provided by the LEA. A student's IEP will most likely be written by a district special educator, assistant principal, Elementary Instructional Specialist, or an administrative designee. The SWD may have an IEP that is directly linked to the IDEA law. In private school, rather than utilizing IEPs, administrators will write and use student learning plans that are comparable to IEPs. SWDs may have learning plans if they attend a private school. Regardless, these students are still covered by the IDEA law. During their K-12 school years, SWDs must have a new psychological evaluation completed every three years.

Academic Adjustments

US universities and other higher education institutions utilize the ADA, yet ADA does not guarantee a specific academic plan (no IEPs) for the implementation of academic accommodations. They often incorporate what they refer to as academic adjustments for their programs. Academic adjustments requested by an SWD may be denied by any US institution, since it may rightfully claim a hardship for providing the accommodation and the university is not obligated to make any changes to its programs.

When an SWD challenges a college or university to receive their accommodations, the process can be daunting. During the K-12 school settings, when a student needs accommodations, the student's parents have the legal right to challenge the school district and have a due process hearing. What happens when an SWD is denied an accommodation in higher education? Due process does not apply because IDEA is no longer the legislative coverage.[33]

Here is a scenario. An SWD requests to have an unreasonable amount, let us say, a two-year extension, to complete a final paper for a semester. Some would say, "That is preposterous!" Here is how this request would go through the university.

- The SWD makes the request to the professor in person and through an email exchange.
- A week goes by and the student follows up, copies the email to the dean of the program, and professor denies the request.
- The student formally contacts the OSA representative. It is recommended that the student provide former written documentation (Evaluations from medical professionals and IEPs) to support their request. Question: did this student receive this support in previous educational settings?

- The OSA representative assists the student by referring to the ADA law and the institution's policies. The student persists and requests a meeting with the dean of the student's program.
- The dean may determine that the request is invalid (squashes the student's request) by citing the institution's current policies on assignments or extensions.

The institution may simply state that the request is a hardship for it, particularly if it is unable to change its curriculum or state-mandated requirements. The university may say it is an unreasonable request, particularly if the request changes the program to a point beyond the university's capacity or ability, and it would have to adapt its program. Therefore, the university may state a hardship in this instance, and the request could end there. The student would concede and either drop the course or hand in the assignment on time with their peers.

However, if the dean accepts the student's request, the university will have to document this case, especially if it resurfaces for this student or other SWDs who make requests similar in nature.

In this case, the student, professor, the OSA representative, and other university advisors for the student must detail a plan for the necessary time needed. Proper arrangements must be made.

If the dean denies the student's request after a formal meeting or hearing for the request, the student may seek legal assistance and challenge the dean's decision. This could take a few weeks (or longer) to resolve, and the semester may end before a decision has been made. If the student feels strongly about needing a particular request and is adamant about receiving this specific accommodation or accommodations, they may believe fighting the institution for their accommodations and education is worth it.

If universities across the nation utilized The Traveling IEP, then more SWDs would receive their appropriate accommodations from faculty, spend more time learning course material, and spend less time challenging institutional officers. The Traveling IEP would serve the student beyond what academic adjustments currently provide because it ensures that the SWD receives exactly the level of support and accommodation they need. The Traveling IEP would increase student retention during college and lead to increased graduation rates among postsecondary SWDs.

CHAPTER FIVE

Concealing Your Disability

Since many postsecondary SWDs choose to conceal their disabilities, they may not have bothered to register with the OSA/Disability since they may have no intention of telling anyone at their university that they have a disability. Many SWDs do not want anyone to know that they have a disability. Furthermore, SWDs tend to hide their disabilities when they transition to college. They have graduated, and they assume that since they have received an official high school diploma, they no longer have their disability. They have shed their disability! Finally! Yet postsecondary SWDs are mistaken. They will grow up and still have their disabilities for the rest of their lives. Whether an SWD is successful in school depends on their adaptive coping strategies.

Figure 4:

Adaptive Coping Strategies for Postsecondary Students with Disabilities

Antecedent of Behavior	Strengths	Resources	Informal Natural Supports	Formal Supports	Desired Result
Stress/anxiety caused when SWD speaks to a professor about an upcoming assignment	Self-efficacy and self-perception, preparation, acquiring information	OSA Assistance with professor connection and institutional policies	Trusted friend on campus, talking, rehearsing possible outcomes	Calling or Zoom session with a parent, OSA assistance, preparing questions for professor	Prepared to confront stressors
Task avoidance or procrastination when SWD has an upcoming assignment	Seek out assistance with scheduling, deadlines, and chunking (tasks into smaller parts)	Campus tutoring and writing services, professor office hours or Zoom sessions	Trusted friend on campus to remind or assist with deadlines	Calling or Zoom session with a parent, professor meeting	SWD meets deadlines

Adaptive Coping Strategies

Adaptive coping strategies are our ability to improve our level of functioning—a healthy way of dealing with stress.[34] In life, especially during college, you will experience stress. Knowing what triggers your stress (deadlines, exams, coursework, lack of sleep, inability to focus, social anxiety) and releasing it is crucial.

Speaking with trusted people, such as friends and family, journaling, getting exercise, and being proactive rather than procrastinating, can reduce your stress and possibly eliminate the problem that is causing the stress.

Postsecondary SWDs may still feel the effects of the social stigma that can contribute to departure. Being an adult student with a disability can often be embarrassing or make students feel insecure as college adults. Students need to adapt very quickly. However, students need to speak up if they need accommodations. Students with disabilities need to be proactive and contact accessibility services on their campus.[35] They are protected by special education laws.

Read Your IEPs!

Many postsecondary SWDs are not educated in their legal protections when they enter college. They probably have not read the components of the IDEA law. It is highly unlikely that they have searched Google for relevant disability laws or scanned the websites for legal protections for their college's accessibility services.[36] They may not even read their IEPs and evaluations to know what accommodations they need.[37]

The Health Insurance Portability Accountability Act (HIPAA) is a federal law imposing certain data privacy and data security requirements concerning medical information.[38] The Health Insurance Portability Accountability Act does not protect a student from having to provide medical documentation to substantiate a request for accommodations under the ADA or Section 504 of the Rehabilitation Act. In other words, the SWD cannot say to the OSA representative, "I have HIPAA rights, so I don't have to tell you my diagnosis." The SWD must tell the OSA/DS representative their diagnosis. And SWDs must back it up with medical records and proof of a disability from a licensed psychologist.

The Family Educational Rights and Privacy Act[39], or FERPA, ensures a student's privacy regarding their disability and diagnosis. Occasionally, an SWD may choose to withhold their disability records from a family member. To helicopter parents, parents who are overly active and protective of their eighteen-year-old adult, FERPA may pose a threat, as they may lose control of their SWD to the student's independence. However, these days many families have various parental dynamics, including stepparents, custody battles with estranged parents, and grandparents and legal guardians. It is not uncommon for a postsecondary SWD to employ their FERPA rights in these instances. Furthermore, SWDs might feel intimidated and unsure about requesting accommodations without disclosing their disability status to their professors. To receive proper student services, it is necessary to disclose their disability to the OSA.

There is a drastic difference between the accommodations provided during high school compared to the academic adjustments provided during an SWD's college program. Figure 5, the High

School Verses College Framework, shows how SWDs were receiving 98% of their accommodations and 78% of their services. This plummeted drastically when students went to college, as they received 23% of their accommodations and less than 6% of their services. [40]

SWDs may want their disabilities to disappear during college, so they wish hard to be like everyone else. If they sit in class and fake it, maybe they can appear to be without their disabilities and become like everyone else in college. But this mentality may eventually harm an SWD. In the long run, the responsible SWD knows that they need their accommodations, so they suck it up and make certain to connect with college campus accessibility services, known as the OSA.

Figure 5:

High School Versus College Framework

High School vs. Higher Education

In K-12, SWDs' teachers have a copy of the IEP prior to the start of the semester.

SWDs are solely responsible for self-disclosing and contacting campus Accessibility Service

K-12 SWD does not need to request specific accommodations since they are explicitly written in the SWDs annual formal IEP

SWDs must request accommodations every time they need an accommodation

During high school, 98% of SWDs received accommodations and faculty support, including academic assistance

Postsecondary SWDs only receive 23% support, including testing accommodations, extra time, reader, or calculator, and 12% tutor

78% received at least one Designated Instructional Support (DIS) service (OT/PT/Speech, life skills) while in high school

Less than 6% of postsecondary SWDs received DIS services

Each SWD must provide written documentation of their disability to the OSA. This documentation would be their recent and current psychological report that the SWD has read, so they know what is written in it. Additionally, their disability documentation includes copies of their IEPs, current and previous. You, the SWD, may wish to contact an OSA representative at your college to see if anything else (such as letters from your principal or psychologist) is needed beyond these two pieces of documentation. SWDs may find it useful to speak to a professor, so check with an OSA officer to arrange a brief meeting.

The accessibility office focuses on grades, academics, tutoring, accommodations such as extra time, small-group assistance, and additional in-school and on-site supports. This is what an SWD should ask and confirm with the OSA and their professors (ahead of time). Yet, with the Traveling IEP, the accommodations would mirror what the student was already previously receiving, so the SWD would have less guesswork and more confidence that they would receive the appropriate accommodations. With the Traveling IEP, postsecondary SWDs would have a smoother transition between high school and college.

CHAPTER SIX

What Students Think Professors Believe

For many postsecondary SWDs, needing accommodations to succeed in academics is not new, and needing academic assistance did not just begin during their senior year of high school. For many students, it may be quite the opposite. They have spent most of their elementary and secondary school hours receiving accommodations. Some SWDs may have had limited school hours in a general education setting and felt unwelcomed when they were mainstreamed.

We all know which students leave their general education classroom to go somewhere. The nondisabled students all lift their eyes from their papers and watch the student leave the room. Having their nondisabled peers watch and wonder affects their perception and self-efficacy (beliefs about themselves). What's more, it influences their beliefs about their success in higher education.[41]

Combatting the Stigma

Learning differences are different from other disabilities, particularly physical disabilities, because of the stigma attached to them. Unfortunately, the stigma of having a nonvisible disability still impacts how nondisabled peers relate to disabled students and may lead to social exclusion. Sometimes, students with learning differences may have had limited social activities if they must attend tutoring. This trend seems to continue during college, where a student may have to forego having pizza with their friends in the student activities center because they must go meet with their tutor. The student must make the decision, with tunnel vision or blinders, and realize, "I am here for my education." They must take a deep breath and know that tutoring takes precedence over pizza.

Creating a balance between college classwork and socializing has affected many SWDs who have difficulty sticking to a schedule, meeting deadlines, and require more time for studying and completing papers. However, this should not deter them. Hopefully, they have a role model to show them the ropes.

Since nondisabled college students tend to be more proactive and independent in searching for school programs and post high school options, they can lead by example. Some SWDs may have older siblings who paved the way and became the exemplar for their younger sibling with a disability, while other SWDs simply had the determination to apply to colleges and were admitted. Having a student or sibling role model glorify the college experience can impact how an SWD perceives their own college experience.

By accessing a student mentor, especially if they happen to be a brother or sister, an SWD could view and acquire a more positive attitude about school and college. Having your big brother share positive stories about college and his or her professors might help an SWD feel more confident. An SWD should pick their mentor's brain and gain some strategies. Remember though, that not everything an SWD sees on their brother's Instagram page is true. It is best for an SWD to talk to them personally.

When I was in college, social media was not a thing. Nobody carried cell phones and gossip was still word of mouth. These days, students are on social media worrying about what other people think of them. Wondering (and worrying) about what others think of you is magnified and advertised to the world. For postsecondary SWDs, the world includes their professors. Aside from the concerns about student self-efficacy (what SWDs think about themselves as college students), they may be concerned about what their professors think of them.

What Professors Think of SWDs

Several SWDs reported that college faculty held non-supportive attitudes and that students perceived that faculty lacked sensitivity toward them since they have a disability.[42] Furthermore, they believed that faculty were skeptical and mistrusting of students with nonvisible disabilities, such as learning disabilities and ADHD.

I have often wondered if my professors trust me and know that I am smart. In one of my classes, we had a ten-question quiz, and I was the only one who got 100% on it. The other students gasped in horror and dismay, and asked me, "How did you (the girl with a learning disability, who was slow, and not as intelligent) get a perfect A+ paper and the rest of us only got B's?" I replied, "I studied."

I had studied. I put the time in, put the definitions on flashcards, studied in the cafeteria, practiced with a peer tutor, and gave myself a pretest…you get the picture. I was very serious about this test. To this day, I remember feeling proud of my accomplishment. In the wake of my achievement, I wondered if my professor had any doubts of my ability and would question the validity of my test. I suspected that this professor could not believe that I was the only one who had scored perfectly on the assessment. Maybe he wondered, "How did a disabled person outperform the nondisabled peers?" When he saw my study cards with the definitions, his eyes went big, and he said, "You're going to do well." However, the reaction of my peers stays with me because it exemplifies the social stigma that remains constant for those with disabilities.

As a result of the stigma that still exists, college administrators and faculty members engage in preventative measures against SWDs enrolling in college. Among college faculty, there is still the belief that SWDs must be solely responsible for their academic success. SWDs were admitted to the university or college program; therefore, they should complete the program in the same manner as their nondisabled peers. Faculty may feel that if SWDs are not able to complete the same program, they should refrain from enrolling or leave the program.

College faculty may be misinformed (or not informed at all) about the student's academic accommodations. Furthermore, faculty tend to be set in their ways and may not choose to make the effort to advance their teaching practices. They have earned their Ph.D., so why should they learn new teaching skills? Because most professors have certain beliefs about the style of their teaching and may be reluctant to alter their instructional techniques. They may not ever have taught SWDs, and consequently, their delivery may be limited to the podium or PowerPoint slides. A participant in my case study stated bluntly, "Sometimes professors are just not very good teachers."[43]

Figure 6:

Example Statements by Faculty

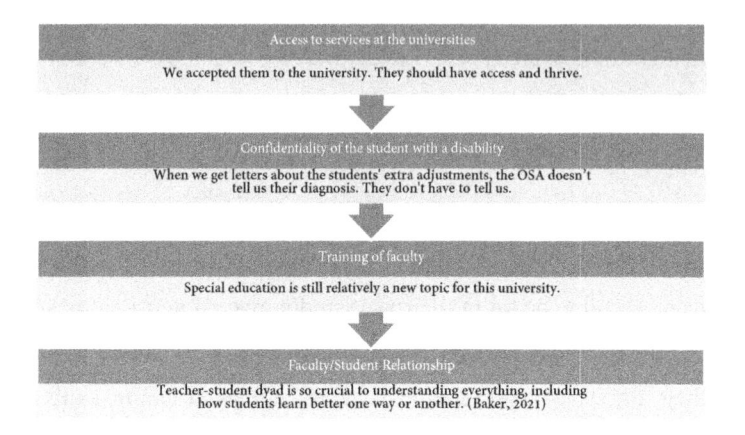

- **Access to services at the universities**
  We accepted them to the university. They should have access and thrive.
- **Confidentiality of the student with a disability**
  When we get letters about the students' extra adjustments, the OSA doesn't tell us their diagnosis. They don't have to tell us.
- **Training of faculty**
  Special education is still relatively a new topic for this university.
- **Faculty/Student Relationship**
  Teacher-student dyad is so crucial to understanding everything, including how students learn better one way or another. (Baker, 2021)

Typical college faculty members do not seek additional training. Figure 6, Example Statements by Faculty, acknowledges the true sentiments of faculty about training. Faculty feel that since they have earned a higher education degree, they are experts in their field. It would be redundant to require additional training from someone who has already established themselves. This is true for college faculty who have never taught. In fact, they may not have had one pedagogy course. A university dean shared with me, "You must remember, *most* professors, not all but *most* professors weren't trained in education, period. They were trained in their field. They weren't trained in pedagogy and even less was there anything on pedagogy about *special education* or *adaptive pedagogy*."[44]

Professors in my case study believed that their institutions could be improved.[45] This is not to say that every single faculty member at any one university is exceeding pedagogical standards in every aspect of their courses. On the contrary, faculty members felt that their colleagues *should* have additional training and place the task of training these professors on university administrators. Furthermore, they put additional pressure on the OSA. One professor told me that if all students are being served and instructed as they should be, "we" (the college) would not need an OSA. Ideally, colleges should not need disability services or OSA. They need trained faculty. Having trained faculty would make all classes (and colleges) accessible.

SWDs are up against the social stigma that has been in existence for decades. SWDs reported feeling a sense of intimidation and rejection. They may feel as though they must demonstrate their ability before they can be accepted into society and in college. Didn't postsecondary SWDs graduate from high school like every other college freshman? Yes, they did. Because of the stigma and the negative perception of SWDs, they must apply and enroll in college, execute effective transition (independently), complete timely registration processes, access the accessibility services unit on campus, and contact the appropriate faculty, among many other procedures, to be considered successful and compete with their nondisabled peers.

The ingrained social stigma about SWDs causes those in power at higher education institutions to have the perception that SWDs do not belong in academic settings. They firmly believe that postsecondary SWDs are not scholars. More than ever, postsecondary SWDs must push forward, challenge the authority at all institutions, and prove them wrong! Postsecondary SWDs *are* scholars!

CHAPTER SEVEN
Faculty Perceptions

A biology professor of undergraduate students was grading papers for a class in which she had two SWDs. She told me, "When I first began as a professor, my students with learning disabilities always passed my class. I always give them C's."

"How come they do not earn A's?" I asked.

In the past, she had always assumed that SWDs must only be capable of earning the minimum grade. However, throughout her years as a professor, she modified her instructional strategies, incorporated Universal Design of Learning (UDL)[46], and discovered that SWDs were very creative and challenged her straight-A students. The biology professor admitted that she had to change her mindset about *all* her students and their abilities. These experiences altered her perception of her SWDs.

Expectations and Misconceptions

College professors may have certain expectations and misconceptions about SWDs. Some professors have negative attitudes toward SWDs based on their misconceptions and being uninformed.[47] For example, they may assume that a student who has ADHD will be disruptive during their class. This could be the case; however, professors may not know that some students with ADHD may be very quiet and choose a seat in the back of the lecture hall or may not even come to class. Regardless, these actions by students with disabilities impact the professor's ability to teach all students. How can new college students alter a professor's pint of view?

Changing the perception of postsecondary SWDs has been a national concern for half a century. Some professors wonder how SWDs got into college. This sarcastic point of view can show itself through a professor's eyeroll, pursed lips, raised brow, exaggerated sigh, and several other nonverbal disapproving actions. Among faculty, there is still a widespread belief that SWDs are incapable of earning a college degree and are not successful with academics, regardless of the accommodations and intervention provided to them.

Believe it or not, some college faculty may even tell you that those with disabilities do not belong in school at all, especially in college. A few professors have stated that they would rather teach all nondisabled students—it is simply easier to have an entire class with students who do not require accommodations and additional support.[48] In the past two years, since the Covid-19 pandemic began in 2020, many professors at colleges and universities nationwide have begun teaching virtually, hybrid, or in person, and all professors have taught or will teach postsecondary SWDs.

There is still a notion (perception) that a college education is for the elite, the gifted, and the fortunate. In 2022 though, most colleges have aimed to address issues of Diversity, Equity, and Inclusion (DEI), but not disability topics. It remains that the negative perception toward postsecondary SWDs is the result of an ingrained stigma in our society. Despite many professors' negative attitudes toward SWDs, the population of SWDs has increased significantly in higher education because of the changes in national special education laws such as the ADA and the IDEA. Disability activists, family members, and SWDs continue to work to reduce and eliminate this cultural phenomenon. Professors are expected to teach them and adhere to these national disability policies. Professors must put their personal beliefs aside.

I'm a professor, not a teacher

For centuries, lecturers and professors have just done that: profess to students who are eager to learn higher academic knowledge. However, in the 21st century, knowledge of technology, skills and trades, and advanced leadership skills must be taught through methods beyond reading PowerPoint slides.

It's assumed that since most professors have earned a Ph.D. or an Ed.D., they have a higher-level degree; therefore, they would not need additional training to teach at a college or university. What is alarming is how many professors may have limited or no teaching experience, so they have difficulty creating and delivering effective lessons."[49] Many college professors have a specialty area, for example, psychology, and did not major in education. As a result, these professors have no formal pedagogical training, especially in special education and disabilities studies.

At many universities around the country, formal disabilities training might not occur. After signing a contract, many college professors are overwhelmed and get started creating their syllabus and ordering books. Some professors go from human resources to setting up their Zoom meeting class schedule and overlook formal new-hire trainings.

It is also widely known that formal training is optional in higher education settings. In contrast to higher education institutions, K-12 school districts are diligent in providing suitable training to all their teachers, including nonspecial educators, which impacts the overall academic success and high school graduation rates of SWDs. During K-12 teacher onboarding with school districts, there are several must-complete modules about diversity, safety, sexual harassment and conduct, and cyberbullying, to name a few. Nationwide, there is no law or mandated requirement for further training of college faculty written in each of their employment contracts. Even if a university does have basic onboarding requirements, such as videos, the content presented is not specifically tailored around disabilities. In higher Ed, there are fewer national mandates that ensure the compliance of professors to serve those with disabilities.

What happens next? Early career or nontenured professors lack experience in teaching and tend to struggle to implement effective teaching strategies. They might not have an education degree, studied pedagogy, studied Bloom's Taxonomy or Addies models of teaching, or any other formal model of instruction.[50] Not only may their delivery of instruction be weak, but new professors may also be unable to provide the appropriate (and legal) accommodations for postsecondary SWDs. This responsibility then falls to the higher education institution.

As it stands, there is a significant correlation between the faculty's limited knowledge of special education law and their willingness to provide accommodations to SWDs.[51] One participant of my case study admitted that he drove to his college campus and attended a luncheon training on UDL.[52] Upon the completion of this training, this professor said he learned a lot but had yet to implement the UDL strategies into his college courses. The reason for his inability to implement the UDL strategies was unclear. He was eager to learn new strategies and thought UDL was interesting, but he was incapable of transferring this new knowledge into action.

Finally, this participant stated that he needed further guidance on applying UDL strategies, but who is responsible for overseeing this professor's development in his lecture class? The dean? And does the dean have the time and resources to oversee every single part-time lecturer at their university? Without laws and policies to enforce the proper training and the implementation of strategies such as UDL, college professors will not have to alter their current manner of instruction and the delivery of academic content.[53]

In addition to content delivery, there is the issue of scaffolding and differentiation. How do you properly accommodate students? Many professors have no idea how to provide accommodations. There is a stark comparison between the accommodations provided in the K-12 setting, which are mandatory, versus the optional accommodations provided in colleges and universities. Academic adjustments that are not accommodations are optional and, therefore, universities may contest these adjustments if they create a hardship for the university.[54] This goes together with faculty perspectives because some faculty hold the belief that since the SWD applied to the college or university, they may be rejected during the admission process. There may be several reasons the SWD was rejected. A student's K-12 education is mandatory, yet higher education is optional. In the end, an SWD should apply to more than one university to maximize their higher education options.

What do faculty really know about disabilities?

In our society, people categorize disabilities based on the severity of the diagnosis. Some categories are mild, while others are severe. These categories are explained in detail in the *Diagnostic and Statistical Manual 5*.[55] However, most people, even Ph.D.s who are experts, have not read this manual cover to cover.

Professors, like most people, tend to be more sympathetic toward those with physical disabilities such as polio or a speech and language disorder, as opposed to a learning disability, such as ADHD.[56] Faculty have more positive attitudes toward students with physical disabilities, but hold more negative attitudes about mental health disabilities and learning disabilities. These attitudes reflect the stigma about learning differences and disabilities. Faculty still maintain uncertainty regarding the qualification for disability services since they are not licensed psychologists and have not read the *DSM 5*. What do they really know about ADHD? They shrug their shoulders. They may know because their son or daughter was diagnosed with ADHD in 2010, but no one would have expected that they have read the *DSM 5* simply because they have earned a doctoral degree. Unless you are well-versed with the *DSM 5*, the realities of those with disabilities may be unknown.

Many professors believe if you look like everyone else, you must learn like everyone else, and this is not necessarily the case. Faculty perceived that the students who received accommodations had an unfair advantage in academic settings. Yet often, students with learning differences simply need extra processing time or the lesson material is explained differently because of a processing delay. I am a perfect example of this. I always need things repeated and explained a few different ways. Then I repeat it back to the professor to make sure that I am correct. Students with disabilities, like me, are perfectly capable of learning the material presented, but they require accommodations, specifically extra time. Faculty attitudes toward postsecondary SWDs varied, depending on the faculty's prior experiences and familiarity with disabilities.

Faculty willingness to provide accommodations varied based on the exact type of accommodation being provided to SWDs. There was a high level of willingness for recorded lectures, extra time, and exam placement relocated to the support services office. However, faculty members were least willing to provide supplementary materials such as an outline of their lecture or assignments in an alternative format.[57]

According to my case study, professors had poor attitudes about spending additional time to support postsecondary SWDs. Faculty felt that if an SWD had been accepted to the university, they must complete assignments at the same time as their nondisabled peers during the semester. This sort of thinking is based on misconceptions and negative attitudes toward SWDs. Additionally, the faculty felt that if the student were admitted to a higher education setting, the student must accept the academic responsibility, despite the new setting and previous learning accommodations.

Which brings me to another point. There are U.S. universities that do not have disability services on campus. Why? Because they do not admit students with disabilities. Some institutions, admission officers and faculty, simply believe that SWDs should not be in college at all and that it diminishes the upstanding reputation of the university.[58] In addition to my personal belief—that all higher education institutions must serve SWDs equally and that a national law should be passed to ensure that IEPs are used in college—I am in shock that there are still colleges and universities that currently have no disability/accessibility services on campus.[59] And that the absence of DS in college is discrimination.

Occasionally, postsecondary SWDs have requested an extension for their assignments beyond the approved calendar semester from their university, and this is not acceptable to professors. Some college professors feel that SWDs should have the same amount of time to do the same amount of coursework as their nondisabled peers. That's only fair...right? This would include SWDs' midterm and final exams. Professors who maintain this point of view may not fully comprehend the scope of SWDs' disabilities. Not only are they unaware of the impact of a disability, but they shy away from the opportunity to learn and develop an authentic understanding of postsecondary SWDs.

When SWDs receive accommodations such as extra time, faculty members may hold negative viewpoints about SWDs' success.[60] Faculty felt that there was an unfair advantage for an

SWD if they had extra time on assignments or exams. There is an incorrect assumption that students who ask for accommodations are looking for an easy way out of intellectual assignments and academic requirements. They even believe that postsecondary SWDs provide excuses. Additionally, faculty perceived that SWDs felt entitled and were taking advantage of the system.

The reason SWDs have accommodations such as extra time is they are diagnosed by a professional psychologist who has determined that with extra time and other accommodations, they will access the university curriculum. This SWD would be able to do the assignments, take the exams, and hand in their final papers on time. *I am* one of these students who require not just extra time, but double time. Furthermore, I also have been authorized to take exams in a separate room to minimize distractions. As a test taker, I need this accommodation since I am so distracted by everyone else taking the test.

During my mid-twenties, I decided to become an English teacher. When I took state credentialing assessments, I registered for seven different assessments that measured different competencies. As I took each exam, one at a time, I passed some of them and failed others. There were usually forty-five multiple choice questions and two very long essays to write about curriculum development, the theory of education, and classroom management. I could not become a licensed teacher until I passed them all. I took the first couple of exams without accommodations, but I knew in my gut I could pass them all if I had extra time. It took me a month to find a psychologist to assess an adult with a learning disability and schedule a two-day testing session. I needed an up-to-date psychological report to determine that, at twenty-eight years old, I still had a learning disability. Upon receiving the accommodations, I passed all my state teacher exams.

Postsecondary SWDs feel relieved and supported when they receive their accommodations. However, there may be college faculty who tend to experience detrimental effects when their students receive extra time. Many professors were dismayed about the student and the situation of needing additional time. When university administrators, especially the OSA officers, addressed the time issue with faculty, they expressed that they had insufficient knowledge and training about providing appropriate accommodations to postsecondary SWDs. Some professors hesitated when instructed to allow an SWD extra time, as it impeded their ability to maintain a schedule for final grades. On one hand, faculty must adhere to the university semester schedule, but then they are instructed that they must be flexible with supporting SWDs. In my study, faculty showed signs of frustration and anxiety and conveyed this to their superiors at their university.

When these professors accepted the additional workload of providing accommodations, they also expressed that they felt that they weren't being supported by their university administrators. Other professors felt that providing extra time to students diminished the academic standard of the university.[61]

As a college professor with learning disabilities, my mission in life became to figure out how to support other college professors and ultimately change their perspectives of postsecondary SWDs.

Changing faculty members' perceptions about providing appropriate accommodations is challenging. We know that how a professor feels about SWDs directly impacts those students and determines whether they continue taking their professor's class. Who wants to take a class when they believe the professor doesn't like and respect them, especially if the professor has made it clear how they feel about them? This would very likely cause a student to drop the class and even depart their college program.

Some college professors ask, "What do I have to do to accommodate a student with a disability so I do not get fired or sued?" Professors may even resent that SWDs may not always provide sufficient notice ahead of time regarding the need for accommodations. In the end, faculty are willing to provide accommodations; however, they lack knowledge of national disability law.

Even with mandated disability legislation, there are still some faculty members who show a disinterest in having to instruct SWDs at all.[62] By addressing these concerns and providing appropriate faculty training, higher education institutions can begin establishing a change in faculty attitudes and perceptions.

It was found that expert special education teachers are guided by their values and principles regarding inclusion. They demonstrate this principle by encouraging collaboration between nondisabled and disabled peers in their classes or virtual settings. In addition, faculty may employ UDL strategies, as they know to focus on their SWDs' strengths and allow them to benefit from inclusive learning and peer encouragement. During virtual learning sessions, online professors may place SWDs in breakout rooms on a Zoom session and facilitate learning through questions posted in the Chat Box. These professors are mindful that these SWDs may require support.

Since we established that faculty may have different beliefs about the type of disability, their attitudes toward the inclusion of SWDs are different, depending on the nature of the disability. Sensitivity toward SWDs is a quality that more faculty need to possess.[63]

As a professor, you have the power to alter your instruction. More importantly, your attitude toward SWDs can influence your delivery of content and the level of support you provide to those students. You may discover that you go above and beyond because you wish to see these students grasp a difficult concept or emerge as authentic scholars. An SWD's academic achievement may increase because of your support. It can even improve their overall GPA.[64]

When college faculty members demonstrated positive attitudes, they were willing to provide accommodations to their

SWDs. When asked to provide the accommodations, they were agreeable to accommodating, even though they may not have had the skills to provide the accommodations. These professors were open and willing to learn.

There are professors, though, who still lack knowledge of the IDEA law and Section 504 of the Rehabilitation Act. Most professors have not researched disability law. Why should they? That is not their specialty or area of expertise. When professors lack knowledge of the disability laws, they struggle to implement the appropriate accommodations. Consequently, these professors must receive support from their institution, particularly the OSA or campus disability services.

Returning to my mission, I want professors to know that they can support SWDs without fear. Professors want to share their knowledge. Why should they be scared? Then they feel guilty about not knowing something because they have a Ph.D., so they feel like they must be an expert in everything and then they become defensive and shut down. Increasing faculty knowledge about disabilities was found to be the precondition for whether faculty would have a positive experience working with SWDs. College faculty should be happy and love their jobs! They should look forward to professing and teaching. Faculty should feel pride knowing they supported all students!

CHAPTER EIGHT
The Value of Mentorship

The most significant way to learn...anything...is by acquiring a mentor. When students have a clear vision of what they want, they more easily obtain it. When students have a model, they are better able to imitate those who are doing what they see themselves doing someday. SWDs can ask questions and receive feedback on projects and become able to formulate a better plan for reaching their end goal. Even if an SWD changes their major, they will have had the opportunity to gain experience, meet people, and eliminate fields that seemed attractive in the past. With the assistance of OSA officers, academic advisors, other campus academic supports (writing and academic tutoring service centers), and invested faculty, SWDs can complete their projected programs—and graduate.

Students who drop out of college are more likely to leave during their freshman year because they get discouraged by their lack of progress and low motivation to continue.[65] When you know where you are going, it is easier to get there. Leadership geniuses, such as Steven Covey and Simon Sinek, will tell you to begin with the end in mind[66] and "dream big. Start small, but most of all, start."[67]

When a student with a disability connects with their faculty members, it inspires them to be curious, become more engaged in academic content, and model them. They see something that resonates within themselves. Ultimately, because they may wish to advance in this field, they view this professor as their mentor.

When SWDs connect with faculty, they have more positive interactions, such as discussing familiar topics and seeking advice from them for their future. By receiving authentic support from a faculty member, an SWD may develop greater independence in the long run. For example, a professor may utilize backward planning and a color-coded grid calendar in conjunction with their syllabus to assist an SWD with assignments that are due. The professor is not required to provide the color-coded calendar, yet they believe it will increase the likelihood that their SWDs will complete assignments and turn the assignments in on time. Even though this task may initially consume a professor's time because they feel strongly that this piece of support is needed, they are glad to do it. If this support is successful, the professor may feel pride, relief, or gratitude; all positive reactions and intrinsic motivation for continuing to provide this support in the future.

Faculty shape students into becoming who they will become. SWDs who feel nurtured attend better to nonpreferred tasks and demonstrate stronger engagement when tasks are difficult. Furthermore, they persevere during challenges and are not afraid to ask questions of the professor. The college-level curriculum is purposefully challenging to increase students' development as a scholar. It is no surprise that postsecondary SWDs have better academic success toward their goals and graduation because they have connected with faculty and developed interpersonal skills.

Not all college faculty perceive assisting SWDs as a time constraint or intrusion. During my case study, I noticed that professors who had family members with disabilities were more sensitive about disabilities than those who were acquainted with those with disabilities. College faculty members with close families with disabilities emanated greater compassion toward other people with disabilities.

One professor had a niece with a disability, and this influenced her to be proactive and show compassion toward an SWD in one of her courses. She decided to reteach her lessons to this SWD in a virtual setting so this student could access the course material on time. Wow! She was amazing. She taught some of her classes twice, once in person for her nondisabled peers, and again on Zoom with her SWD. She is a hero and extremely aware of the need to support those with disabilities. These attributes, sensitivity, and compassion strengthened faculty members' connections with SWDs.

More supportive attitudes were found by professors who made direct contact with SWDs and those who engaged in training. Professors who nurtured SWDs provided an increased level of support that benefitted them. When faculty choose to provide support to SWDs by altering their methods of delivery and assessment and providing the necessary supports, such as meeting for office hours or providing one-to-one additional instruction, SWDs meet the same standards as their nondisabled peers.[68] Faculty benefit from knowing precisely what their responsibilities were toward SWDs, and many wanted to give additional time and help. Faculty demonstrate a strong interest in professional development opportunities related to college SWDs.[69] When professors care and show authentic compassion toward SWDs, the result is positive for both SWDs and faculty.

Faculty who demonstrated compassion toward SWDs believe SWDs are creative and powerful and have a bright future ahead of them. Because faculty have had good experiences with SWDs, they have a positive perception of them. As a result of this positivity, professors are willing and can accommodate SWDs.[70]

There are many reasons SWDs leave college. Mainly though, the SWD cannot self-advocate for their academic needs. Without knowing their rights and communicating their needs to appropriate OSA officers, SWDs risk not receiving accommodations. SWDs may fail to communicate with university faculty.[71] SWDs who established a relationship with their professors demonstrated far greater academic success and advancement in their higher education programs. The elements of academic integration and positive interactions with faculty would greatly enhance the overall academic success of SWDs, as faculty influence the amount of time spent in an academic program of study. Each SWD's disability status is recognized on a case-by-case basis.

Professors who have proved successful in instructing postsecondary SWDs have demonstrated positive attitudes and expressed the belief that SWDs can flourish if provided the appropriate accommodations.

CHAPTER NINE

Tailored Disability Training for College Faculty

Even though there has been a spike of diversity training scattered throughout colleges across the country, disability training is still scarce. In recent years, there has been a significant increase of minority populations represented at colleges, particularly those of African American and Latinx populations.[72] College administrators indicated that their institutions were not prepared for the demographic shift, sharing concerns of training for faculty in cultural differences, creating departments to address this need for more cultural awareness, and establishing procedures to create a multicultural campus. The issue of reforming culturally responsive college campuses to resolve the need for greater diversity leads to the issue of forming disability training to rectify this for university faculty.

Faculty and Institutions' Reservations

A specific tailored training in disabilities and disability law for professors that covers laws such as the ADA needs to be developed and implemented at every university nationwide. For disability compliance to be fully recognized on a national level, the concept of disabilities training (not just diversity training) must be accepted by university leaders and enforced at all colleges and universities nationwide.

Enforcing a national special education training for faculty in higher education is complex. Institutional management and administration on all college campuses and programs alike must have buy-in to this action. Additionally, they would be tasked with monitoring and supervising faculty and their training to ensure the legal compliance for postsecondary SWDs. There would be more advanced questions regarding the proper evaluation of instructors. Holding each university accountable for such programs would be an arduous task.

In a K-12 setting, administrators of LEAs must oversee special education instruction and monitor for effective implementation of their programs. Furthermore, merely training faculty on effective classroom strategies does not guarantee the proper implementation of such practices.

Currently, the evaluation of highly effective special education K-12 teachers includes the evaluation of their performance in addition to legal compliance and implementation of direct, explicit instruction.[73] These measures are heavily monitored by school district representatives, research-based, and evaluated routinely to ensure compliance with special education in every K-12 school district. Measures such as a District Validation Review act as checks and balances to monitor special education services.[74]

In higher education though, there are fewer national mandates to ensure that accommodations are provided to SWDs per the ADA law, and faculty training is optional. Once a faculty member is hired by a university, they have certain academic and university responsibilities, but none of these responsibilities include additional training. Some professors may not particularly want SWDs in their courses and express this preference to university administration, as if they alone can determine each student's academic fate. However, there are various compliance measures that are left up to each institution.

If there are grievances at universities, there are consequences for professors' actions. Some college faculty may be on probation for failing too many SWDs. Others neglect to comply with the OSA's requests, deeming their demands impossible to meet. Since professors feel that since they have earned higher education degrees, Ph.D.s and Ed.D.s, they are experts and, therefore, do not need further training in disability studies. Yet this notion is contrary to research-based claims and by higher education faculty.

According to my case study, participants stated that not providing the appropriate accommodations was a result of insufficient knowledge and training. Among faculty surveyed, 100% reported that they would like to have further training and that they needed it from their universities. Specifically, faculty need to recognize the changes to the curriculum; they need to accept that they will need to provide accommodations to SWDs and improve their instructional techniques.

However, at this time, higher education institutions have the prerogative to decide which program modifications they are willing to accept, and which accommodations and academic adjustments will cause the least hindrance within their programs. Finally, the specific trainings offered to faculty is determined by university boards and administrators.

Tailored Disability Training

Higher education faculty may be uneducated in higher education disability laws and institutional policies that pertain to SWDs. As I stated earlier, most professors have a specialty area, and this area may be miles away from disability policy. Since recent disability policy reflects the need for instructional accommodations in all educational settings, including college, it would be beneficial for higher education faculty to understand the correlating laws.

A tailored disability training could be accomplished by the university, the OSA, or by outsourcing knowledgeable disability representatives and consultants. Even if the tailored disability training would be presented to protect new and existing faculty at any given university, it would inform professors of their duties when serving SWDs, it would protect them from frivolous grievances from SWDs, and it would allow professors to know the current institutional policies at their place of employment.

Current Policies and Procedures

Since universities and colleges in the U.S. have a campus disabilities office, OSA, or a disability services representative, disability policy (and training) responsibility has been placed on these offices. Higher education institutions and their policies are overseen by state legislature, the governor, and various regulatory or coordinating agencies. However, policy makers have limited power in higher education.

State institutions may choose to participate in national organizations that achieve advocacy and policy goals. As organizations regulate diversity and other related policies at the university level that may be more complex in nature, board members and other stakeholders would advise and implement program changes for postsecondary SWDs. These changes could include disability training for faculty.

Both SWDs and professors should be aware of these current procedures. At many universities, colleges, and community colleges, an SWD will have to provide a new semester request form each semester to the OSA and to each professor to inform them of their necessary accommodations. It would be wise for an

SWD to check with professors personally ahead of time, prior to the first day of class. This way, the professor can confirm that they received the SWD's letter of accommodations and exam needs.

The OSA may send email to the professor. Be mindful, some professors do not receive or open their email before the first day of class. It is best to receive a verbal acknowledgement from each professor. This will give the SWD an opportunity to connect with each of their professors. Many SWDs face the challenge of establishing positive faculty interaction.[75] Often SWDs exhibit stress because of having to address and interact with professors. They may fear that their professors will alienate them and tag them as unintelligent. Remember, as an SWD, you do not have to disclose your diagnosis to your professor, but if you want to receive your accommodations as you deserve them, you must convey the exact accommodations that you need to succeed in college as an SWD.

Based on what you have read in this book, postsecondary SWDs must realize that faculty may not know about disabilities. SWDs may know more about their disabilities and how they learn than their professors. Furthermore, SWDs know what has worked for them during school in the past. With the Traveling IEP and tailored disability training, college faculty can gain valuable information about SWDs and how they learn, why they need each accommodation in their IEPs, and how to deliver effective instruction to promote success toward college graduation. Tailored disability training goes together with the Traveling IEP.

The bigger issue for university administrators, legislators, and everyone else is what the IEP looks like in college.

CHAPTER TEN

The Traveling IEP

In 2008, the HEOA[76] passed and stated that colleges should meet the academic needs of postsecondary SWDs. However, the HEOA, or any other piece of legislation aside from the ADA, has not been accepted or adopted by US colleges and universities. They still use the ADA from 1973. On a national level, the IDEA has been updated twice, in 1990 and in 2004. Yet no piece of solid legislation that specifically serves postsecondary SWDs has been implemented.

Section 504 and the HEOA

During the past fifty years, a few pieces of disability legislation have been passed by Congress, and it was assumed that the appropriate support was provided to postsecondary SWDs. However, these pieces of legislation have not served postsecondary SWDs as they should have. Therefore, disability advocates are still fighting to provide better supports to postsecondary SWDs.

Specific pieces of legislation include the Rehabilitation Act that mandated federal protection against the discrimination of people (not specifically postsecondary SWDs) with disabilities from any program that receives federal funds.[77] Section 504 forbids discrimination and allows access; however, it does not have a detailed academic plan that promotes success toward graduation. Allow me to translate the Rehabilitation Act: Section 504 allows a postsecondary student with a disability access into the college classroom and forbids discrimination from the university; however, it does not mean that the professor (or all professors) who teaches the course is going to know how to instruct the SWD so that they can succeed, thrive academically, and graduate from college. The how is Specially Designed Instruction that would be explicitly detailed in each college student's Traveling IEP.

In August of 2008, the HEOA was amended to extend the Higher Education Act of 1965. Title VII of the HEOA reauthorization was passed and sought to provide postsecondary SWDs with greater academic support and mainly to train faculty. The HEOA explicitly expressed that professional development was needed and would be provided to faculty, staff, and administrators at higher education institutions. The HEOA would employ innovative, effective, and efficient teaching methods and strategies. Institutions will provide faculty, staff, and administrators with the skills and supports necessary to teach and meet the academic needs of SWDs. The training specified in the HEOA would improve the retention of such students in postsecondary education.[78]

The problem with the HEOA is it exists as solid legislation, yet higher education institutions (and their administrators) have not accepted it as official disability legislation for US universities. Therefore, the HEOA is not being employed. Many people do not even know the HEOA exists. Higher education institutions in the United States are not utilizing the HEOA, but rather defaulting to the ADA as their official disability legislation.

Introducing the RISE Act

Not until 2021 was there any national notoriety of legislation for postsecondary SWDs. On February 5, 2021, Colorado Representative Diana DeGette introduced H.R. 869 *Research Investment to Spark the Economy Act of 2021* (RISE) to Congress.[79] Initially, the RISE Act was introduced to promote research efforts to remedy the effects of the Coronavirus Disease 2019 (Covid-19) pandemic. Its purpose was to provide financial support, in the form of research grants, to several national departments, including the Department of Education. Each department would conduct research to support graduate and undergraduate students, postdoctoral students, principal investigators, and administrative and technical support staff.

In July 2021, Pennsylvania Senator Bob Casey Jr. introduced the Respond, Innovate, Support, Empower Act that focused on providing greater assistance for postsecondary SWDs.[80] This bill aimed to amend the Higher Education Act of 1965 to provide SWDs and their families with access to critical information needed to select the right college and succeed once enrolled. Additionally, it addressed the critical component of supporting postsecondary SWDs that had been missing in other legislation.

The RISE Act proposed by Senator Casey was a clearer shot at having IEPs be approved documentation for postsecondary SWDs. Still, colleges would be responsible and held accountable for accommodating SWDs. This bill could have led to tremendous breakthroughs for postsecondary SWDs.

I felt compelled to act! Figure 7 shows the substantial Op-Ed article that I wrote for *PennLive*, titled, "Senator Casey is Right! Congress Needs to Help College Students With Disabilities."[81] I spent hours researching and presented a policy brief to the Tom Ridge Policy Group and the National Organization on Disability. I didn't stop there. Next, I took the opportunity to promote the RISE Act because I feel so strongly about having the Traveling IEP in college, so I contacted and I met with Senator Casey's office.

The article in Figure 7 first illustrated this concept of having a national law that enforced all colleges to use IEPs. I was happy to highlight Senator Robert Casey since his progress in this bill was directly aligned with my mission. Yet over the summer months of 2021, to my disappointment, there was no activity beyond the Introduction stage. Casey's office representative reminded me that changes in legislation could take years.

Figure 7:
Article Published in PennLive

Sen. Casey is right: Congress needs to help college students with disabilities | Opinion

Published: Aug. 06, 2021, 9:05 a.m.
By <u>Guest Editorial</u>
By Toby Tomlinson Baker, Ph.D.

I have been an early and outspoken advocate, in the pages of PennLive and elsewhere, for the concept of improving support for students with disabilities during K-12 and extending these supports to college. While this may seem to be a useful, even obvious, policy, it has "fallen between the cracks" of federal legislation and the uneven administration at the college and university level.

I am happy to say that Sen. Robert Casey has incorporated this concept into his newly reintroduced legislation referred to as the RISE (Respond, Innovate, Support, and Empower) Act. While this legislation covers a number of topics, I want to point particularly to the fact it provides for the "travel" of the Individual Education Plans (IEP's) from high school to college and requires higher education institutions to honor them. As I have pointed out in my writing on this topic, it is time for colleges and universities to have consistency and to achieve the high standard that, under the RISE Act, would be mandated.

We all know students with disabilities, and we may even know a student with a disability who has graduated from high school and is transitioning to college this fall, either in-person or virtually. A crucial aspect of their transition to college is knowing their Individual Education Plan or IEP.

College freshman with disabilities may have previously had Individualized Education Plans, or IEPs when they were in K-12 schools. Since transitioning to college, their IEPs have been discontinued and are no longer active because IEPs do not "travel" to college with students with disabilities. Higher education institutions in the United States do not honor IEPs or individual student accommodations as specified by the Individuals with Disabilities Education Act (IDEA).

But recently, Sen. Bob Casey (D-PA) introduced the RISE Act which focuses on assisting students with disabilities in higher education. Not only with the IEP be approved documentation, but colleges would be responsible and accountable for accommodating students with disabilities.

Most universities utilize the ADA. The ADA does not guarantee a specific academic plan (No IEPs) for the implementation of academic accommodations. Furthermore, colleges often incorporate what they refer to as "academic adjustments" for their programs. Academic adjustments requested by an SWD may be denied by any U.S. institution since it may rightfully claim a hardship for providing the accommodation and the university is not obligated to make any changes to their programs.

Ironically, a separate and more recent law, the Higher Education Opportunity Act from 2008 (HEOA) states that institutions and faculty will meet the academic needs of postsecondary SWDs. However, the HEOA has not been accepted or adopted by U.S. colleges and universities and they still use the ADA. Consequently, postsecondary students with disabilities may not be receiving the accommodations that they need and deserve.

But the RISE Act will change this for colleges and institutions! The rise act will make it possible for is student's IEP to be utilized as approved documentation during college.

But how hard can it be to provide an accommodation to a college student with a disability? Many people assume that college professors would be extremely knowledgeable in providing appropriate accommodations to all their students. Yet, that is not the case. In fact, at most universities, faculty training is *optional*, not required. But the RISE Act authorizes more funding, research, and resources to support postsecondary students with disabilities.

This month, Sen. Casey reintroduced a bill that should be passed! It's our job to urge our Congressional representatives to pass the RISE Act to be utilized by all U.S. colleges and universities. Colleges and universities should welcome this policy because it allows them to achieve a higher standard.

In February, I recorded a webinar about IEPs and transition with the President of the Learning Disabilities Association of America. Despite promotional activity done by disabilities activists, lobbyists, and nonprofit groups such as Learning Disabilities Association of America, the RISE Act remained stagnant in its status as Introduced. Table 1 lists the most recent legislative activity promoting the IEP to be used as official documentation in higher education settings.

Table 1:

U.S. Legislators and Status of Bills That Promote the IEP in Higher Education

Legislator	State/Party	Piece of Legislation	Date Introduced	Outcome
Diana DeGette	D-CO	H.R. 869 The RISE Act	February 5, 2021	Introduced
Sen. Bob Casey	D-PA	S.2550 The RISE Act	July 29, 2021	Introduced
Rep. Mark DeSaulnier	D-CA	H.R. 7780 (IH) Education and Labor's Mental Health Matters	May 16, 2022	Introduced

Even though measures with the RISE Act remained inactive and it is only in the first stage of legislation, Senator Casey progressed in his cause for supporting SWDs. On January 11, 2022, Senator Casey introduced a new bill, the Safe Equitable Campus Resources and Education Act, which addresses safety and crime on campus involving SWDs. Then, on February 9,

Senator Casey introduced a new bill, Fostering Success in Higher Education Act that addresses foster and homeless youth. Even though these bills support causes supporting postsecondary SWDs, neither of the bills introduced this year specifically focus on IEPs and the support needed for academic success and increased graduation rates. Senator Casey has proposed actions to amend the ADA urging the Department of Justice to ensure websites and information and communication technology are accessible to people with disabilities. Senator Casey has demonstrated consistent actions supporting those with disabilities, and I hope he and his colleagues will continue to act on behalf of postsecondary SWDs.

In May of 2022, California Congressman Mark DeSaulnier reintroduced the concept of greater support for students with disabilities in the Education and Labor's Mental Health Matters Package.[82] Until a bill is passed that allows for greater support for postsecondary SWDs, hence the Traveling IEP, and the law is changed for all colleges and universities, higher education institutions have the right to adjust accommodations to suit the university's needs first and deny any accommodation request made by a postsecondary SWD.

Faculty's Hesitation for The Traveling IEP

To provide equal access to postsecondary SWDs, faculty must understand accommodations for SWDs that align with disability law. This would mean that professors understand certain crucial components that are detailed in IEPs for SWDs, but do professors want IEPs in college? According to my study, nine out of fourteen (65%) professors stated Yes to universities and colleges having IEPs in every state in the US. More than half of these faculty members agree and comprehend that there is an urgency to provide greater support to postsecondary SWDs.

How are all professors going to become well-versed in reading IEPs and understanding disability law in addition to their specific expertise? They are not expected to become certified special education teachers.

Questions about the implementation of such procedures at universities were raised among faculty. US institutions (and their officers) have protested accepting radical measures that would alter their existing programs. However, these measures and the changes that will occur are necessary if all students in the nation are to receive appropriate and equal accommodations to higher education.

OSA

The OSA departments, in general, are doing an exceptional job serving students and training faculty. This is especially true regarding the circumstances from the Covid-19 pandemic. However, OSA departments in all states need additional resources. Because of the additional costs that universities would incur for more training, there should be a federal program to provide funds to all universities to support disability training for faculty.

Purposeful disabilities training is needed at every university, college, community college, and post high school program, and all professors should have the ultimate confidence that they are competent and trained to teach SWDs. This can be accomplished with nationally funded training programs that include:

- Past and current disability policy measures pertinent to universities
- Self-evaluation/teaching strategies, build self-esteem, confidence, self-awareness, and self-efficacy of faculty
- Offer and develop researched-based strategies for better classroom instruction of postsecondary SWDs; and
- Offer solutions to university administrators to create a sophisticated policy structure.

Even though there are fundamental steps that many universities and colleges have taken to address disability awareness, there is still much hesitation from higher education institutions, policy makers, and faculty. Faculty have expressed hesitation to having IEPs in college. There main concerns were:

- SWDs' privacy
- Students' privacy was addressed in Chapter 4. SWDs will perform better and head toward graduation if they self-disclose and receive their accommodations.
- Lack of knowledge of special education

- Disability training is needed as explained in Chapters 9 and 10.
- No current standard for IEPs in college

The biggest concern for faculty was envisioning IEPs in college. What does that look like for universities and faculty? Faculty fear change to the university structure and changes in policies. Additionally, they fear it would diminish the academic standards of the university; yet, to the contrary, serving all students would expand the university standards. At this time, as there is limited legislation supporting individualized education for postsecondary SWDs, the vision of such programs on a national level has yet to be determined. Until legislators enact law to support postsecondary SWDs that include implementing and utilizing the IEP for all SWDs, this vision remains a vision.

The Vision of the Traveling IEP

In the US, students in K-12 schools are entitled to be evaluated and served under the IDEA law. Why not extend this service of the IEP to all SWDs, including those entering college? Allowing IEPs to travel to college would reduce students' stress of wondering if they will be accommodated appropriately during college. It will reduce the mystery and provide a clearer understanding for families and postsecondary SWDs. There has been a sharp increase of SWDs entering colleges and universities; therefore, the likelihood that professors are teaching SWDs is high.

Most higher education administrators agree that placing the burden of all tasks related to disabilities on the OSA is unreasonable. Some universities and colleges do not have the funds, resources, or personnel to meet the demands of their SWDs. By having knowledgeable disability specialists' support at each university department, faculty can seek assistance within their departments rather than seeking help strictly at the OSA. Twenty years ago, a demand for disability specialists would have been scoffed at by university officers and legislators since there were not as many SWDs attending college. However, in this post-Covid decade of vast educational changes, professors must recognize the urgency to alter their instruction, seek in-depth understanding of their students, and be open to learning opportunities.

Institutions should hire and expand on their academic assistance for postsecondary SWDs. Special education consultants, whose specialty is in disability law and application, are recommended for higher education institutions in the US. Moreover, special education consultants would specifically address the needs of each university department and faculty member. Professors should not have run to the OSA every time they have a question. At some universities, there may only be one representative at the OSA or disability office. Professors should have the knowledge from their disability training and have access to an available disability specialist within their department.

Allowing IEPs to be utilized in college does not mean that each professor must study case law or read the entire IDEA piece of legislation (ADA) to teach their class. Just because a professor does not agree or approve of the IEP process does not mean that it does not work. In fact, IEPs work very well. The United States is the leader of the world in special education services for SWDs.[83]

Instead of searching for reasons to disprove IEPs' effectiveness, why not extend this concept to all levels of education? By extracting exactly what professors need to know about special education and Specially Designed Instruction, all colleges and universities could appropriately accommodate all students.

Actionable Steps

There are many services that are missing from college settings that were provided to SWDs previously during their K-12 settings. These accommodations go beyond basic accommodations that may be offered through a 504 Plan, such as providing extra time and smaller settings.

In a K-12 setting, when I write an IEP for a student, in the Free Appropriate Public Education section of their IEP, I write using more personal language that specifies a learning plan designed for that one student. As demonstrated in Figure 8, the Box of Traveling IEP Accommodations, the service of crafting the Specially Designed Instruction for each student with a disability should travel to the university level.

As shown in Figure 8, there are many accommodations that may be used and added or removed depending on the student's needs that year. This is determined by the IEP team that often includes the student. Accommodations can be amended as needed and the student does not have to wait any length of time to receive any of these accommodations that are written in his/her IEP. The IEP protects the student and their education.

Figure 8:

Box of the Traveling IEP Accommodations

Differentiation of instruction, scaffolding, preferential seating, UDL strategies, chunking, or breaking down activities, extra time to complete tasks, repetition, visual scaffolds, graphic organizers, writing drafts prior to the final grade, visuals, models of papers, expectations, copies of professors' PowerPoints ahead of time, expectations described prior to the task, different testing room with proctor, assistive technology, directions read in different way, modified assignment or modified testing, hands-on assignment and increased creativity options, adapted curriculum, pair activities, peer assistance, small-group tasks and instruction, professors who offer a schedule within the syllabus, tasks into smaller parts, break down the steps of the assignment, engaging SWDs.

Rebuilding the university structure to better suit postsecondary SWDs seems like an onerous task, and yet rebuilding is necessary in these upcoming times. Administrators and stakeholders need to recognize that education is constantly changing and with those changes come greater opportunities for postsecondary SWDs. This is the chance and the time for universities and colleges to step up and be part of a great movement that better serves this population of students. It is the responsibility of higher education institutions in this country to advance their thinking, their instructional programs, and train their faculty so they emerge as exceptional institutions of learning for all students, including postsecondary SWDs.

Conclusion

With a deeper understanding of disabilities gained through further training, we can change faculty members' mindsets about teaching postsecondary SWDs. Together, university officers, scholars, and faculty can develop better strategies for instructing SWDs. SWDs can achieve greater academic success in college and graduate.

By connecting with faculty and changing their perspectives on postsecondary SWDs, they can provide better accommodations to postsecondary SWDs. SWDs will see higher graduation rates and become part of the percentage of postsecondary students who graduate from college!

CHAPTER ELEVEN

Graduate Students with Disabilities

To get a master's degree in education or an M.Ed., I had to earn an undergraduate degree. Since I had earned a bachelor's in fine arts, I had earned an undergraduate degree; therefore, I could go to graduate school. Students with disabilities must first earn undergraduate degrees in some discipline to go to graduate school. Unless they finish and earn an undergraduate degree, they will not elevate to master's or doctoral status.

Ph.D.s With Learning Disabilities/ADHD

Currently, there are few academic scholars with learning disabilities. Less than 1% of SWDs earn doctoral degrees.[84] SWDs required IEPs and accommodations during high school, and they succeeded because they had the support they needed. They may still require assistance during college. As I wrote my dissertation, I kept this statistic in mind. As I began examining academic literature, I gasped when I realized there were very few graduate scholars like me. There were limitations to scholarly research for and about SWDs.

When I conducted searches for research articles, what surfaced were dated articles that restated generalizations about SWDs in K-12 settings. Then I found articles that shared results that were inconclusive with mediocre recommendations. There were a few articles by brave researchers, many of whom I cited. They examined real SWDs and asked research questions that seeped into the realm of uncomfortable and probed beyond reasonable academic knowledge. Sometimes, as is the case with solving problems for those with disabilities, there is no clear solution or law to address it.

I found limited academic research articles produced by scholars with disabilities. I did not see myself in any of these research articles. I read several articles about students dropping out of college, not being able to find jobs, and having to move in with their parents for support. I had not dropped out of college, I graduated. I lived with roommates in apartments until I got married, and I have held down a job ever since I was fourteen years old. Yes—fourteen (McDonald's and babysitting count). Postsecondary graduate SWDs were barely mentioned in a few articles among thousands available online. I resented that my population—successful postsecondary students earning Ph.D.s—was not anywhere!

This topic became my mission! I had to discover why so many SWDs were dropping out, and furthermore, what I could do to solve this massive problem in special education. I reached out to a professor at Pepperdine who oversaw academic publishing. When I began writing my first literature review in early 2018, I asked her, "How do I write in my literature review that I have found virtually nothing about postsecondary SWDs?" She replied, "This lack of data fuels your argument that we need more!" Ah-ha! The lack of scholarly research of the topic, graduate SWDs, not only needed to be respectfully acknowledged on a small level, but rather demanded academic attention. I decided to write about postsecondary SWDs explicitly to contribute to the academic research.

My work, my published dissertation, has advanced the greater disability movement. The more I contribute through writing Op-Eds and news articles and publishing in disability and education magazines, the greater the impact becomes toward lessening the stigma about postsecondary SWDs. Years ago, I started presenting my research at conferences, shared at poster sessions, and spoke at webinars. I also wrote policy briefs and presented them to legislators who support my cause. I continue to connect with scholars, legislators, and educators around the country.

Many postsecondary SWDs (who had IEPs) don't see themselves as academics and scholars, and that needs to change. I am proud that I have earned a Ph.D. I discovered that with more education, I was offered higher-paying jobs with greater responsibility. My dream is for other SWDs to overcome their fear and know that they can become scholars too. The Traveling IEP should be utilized during graduate school in addition to undergraduate programs. There must be more graduate SWDs going to college and finishing!

SWDs should not feel that they are less intelligent than other scholars. Moreover, SWDs should never accept the stigma that they are not worthy of earning higher education degrees. SWDs should not have to prove repeatedly their value as scholars. They are worthy of being accepted into top universities, earning graduate degrees, and competing with nondisabled peers for the best jobs. All students with disabilities will get their needed accommodations, at any college or university in the country, because of the Traveling IEP.

RESOURCES

Below is a list of some books I read and professors who influenced me. These professors taught me in the beginning of my journey as I became a leader, scholar, and Ph.D. Just a note, not all these books are disability related, but still are relevant to my professional growth as a graduate student and postsecondary student with a disability. There are so many books, academic journal articles (listed in the References), professors, and leaders that made me who I am today. I will always be grateful for all their wisdom. This list will be a brief version of my favorites. You can always check out my website at https://tobytomlinsonbaker.net for additional resources.

BOOKS

1. Stephen Covey - *7 Habits of Highly Effective People*
2. Linda Darling - Hammond *Preparing Teachers for Deeper Learning*
3. Viktor Frankl - *Man's Search for Meaning*
4. Paulo Freire - *Pedagogy of the Oppressed*
5. Helen Lester - *Author*

6. Ken Robinson - *Creative Schools*
7. Howard Schultz, Dori Jones Yang - *Pour Your Heart Into It*
8. Simon Sinek - *Start with Why*
9. Spencer Johnson - *Who Moved My Cheese?*
10. Dan Zadra - *Where Will You Be Five Years from Now?*

Media and Disability-Related Articles

Baker, T. T. (2022, July). Ph.D.'s with ADHD. *Exceptional Needs Today, Issue 2.* (In Progress).

Baker, T. T. (2022, February 9). The Voice: The Value of Educators with Disabilities. *California Teachers Association.* https://www.cta.org/educator/posts/the-value-of-educators-with-disabilities

Baker, T. T. (2022, February). Strategies to Improve Teaching Students With Speech and Language Impairments During a Mask Mandate. *exceptionalneedstoday.com.* https://www.exceptionalneedstoday.com/post/strategies-to-improve-teaching-students-with-speech-and-language-impairments-during-a-mask-mandate

Baker, T. T. (2021, November). Why College Students with Disabilities Need to Connect with Faculty. *Exceptional Needs Today, Issue 6.* https://exceptionalneedstoday.com/exceptional-needs-today-magazine-november-2021/

Baker, T. T. (2021, August 6). Senator Casey is Right: Congress Needs to Help College Students with Disabilities. *PennLive; Harrisburg Patriot News.*
https://www.pennlive.com/opinion/2021/08/sen-casey-is-right-congress-needs-to-help-college-students-with-disabilities-opinion.html

Baker, T. T. (2021, July 28). What Teachers Can Do to Support Writers with Learning Disabilities. *LDA Today.*
https://ldaamerica.org/lda_today/what-teachers-can-do-to-support-writers-with-learning-disabilities/

Baker, T. T. (2021, June 26). Getting to Know the STEM Media Makers and Global Change Makers at IC4! *Scientific Teen.*
https://www.thescientificteen.org/post/getting-to-know-the-stem-media-makers-and-global-change-makers-at-ic4

Baker, T. T. (2021, May 19). Here's How to Help College Students with Disabilities. *PennLive; Harrisburg Patriot News.*
https://www.pennlive.com/opinion/2021/05/heres-how-to-help-college-students-with-disabilities-opinion.html

Baker, T. T. (2021, May). The Vanishing IEP. *Exceptional Needs Today, Issue 2.*
https://exceptionalneedstoday.com/exceptional-needs-today-magazine-may-2021/

Baker, T. T. (2020, October 14). Self-Advocacy and Success for Postsecondary Students with Disabilities. *LDA Today*. https://ldaamerica.org/lda_today/self-advocacy-and-success-for-postsecondary-students-with-disabilities/

Baker, T. T. (2020, August, 25). *Not-So-Distant Learning, Bringing Students Together, Even When Apart. Newsroom, Pepperdine University.* https://gsep.pepperdine.edu/newsroom/2020/08/not-so-distant-learning-bringing-students-together-even-when-apart/

Baker, T. T. (2020, July 7). Not-So-Distant Learning, Bringing Students Together, Even When Apart. *PennLive; Harrisburg Patriot News.* https://www.pennlive.com/opinion/2020/07/not-so-distant-learning-bringing-students-together-even-when-apart-opinion.html

Baker, T. T. (2020, February 24). Former Student Received Harrison Sylvester Award. *DVFS Website*. Posted 02/24/2020 03:16PM

Baker, T. T. (2020, January 20). Self-Advocacy and Success for Postsecondary Students with Disabilities. *Learning Disabilities Association of America (LDA).* https://ldaamerica.org/lda_today/self-advocacy-and-success-for-postsecondary-students-with-disabilities/

Baker, T. T. (2019, July 17). Congress must pass new laws to ensure students with learning disabilities get support in college. *PennLive.com.* https://www.pennlive.com/opinion/2019/07/congress-must-pass-new-laws-to-ensure-students-with-learning-disabilities-get-support-in-college-opinion.html

Baker T. T. (2018, June). China and the Missing Students with Special Needs. *West Chester Daily Local News.* https://www.dailylocal.com/opinion/letter-to-editor-china-and-missing-students-with-special-needs/article_02f9729e-1214-587e-8a5d-b3cc672df77e.html

Howell, L., & Baker, T. (2018 June 15). Former DV Student Shares Impact of D.V.F.S. Education on her Career. *DVFS Website.* Posted 06/15/2018 03:16PM

REFERENCES

Adreon, D., & Durocher, J. S. (2007). Evaluating the college transition needs of individuals with high-functioning autism spectrum disorders. *Intervention in School and Clinic, 42*(5), 271–279. https://doi.org/10.1177/10534512070420050201https://doi.org/10.1177/10534512070420050201

The ASHA leader, (2018, February 1). Graduation Rate for U.S. Students With Disabilities Hits 65.5 Percent. Vol. 23, Issue 2. https://doi.org/10.1044/leader.NIB4.23022018.16

Baker, T. T. (2021). *Support for students with disabilities: How awareness and accommodations differ across faculty members within the postsecondary context* (Order No. 28539983). Available from ProQuest Dissertations & Theses Global. (2543424985).

Bailey, A. B., & Smith, S. W. (2000). Current topics in review: Providing effective coping strategies and supports for families with children with disabilities. *Intervention in School and Clinic, 35*(5), 294-296.

https://journals.sagepub.com/doi/pdf/10.1177/105345120003500507

Bandura, A. (1977). Self-efficacy: Toward a unifying theory of behavioral change. *Psychological Review, 84*(2), 191–215.

Bandura, A. (1997). *Self-efficacy: The exercise of control.* WH Freeman.

Bays, D. A. (2001). *Supervision of special education instruction in rural public-school districts: A grounded theory* [Doctoral dissertation, Virginia Tech].

Black, R. D., Weinberg, L. A., & Brodwin, M. G. (2014). Universal design for instruction and learning: A pilot study of faculty instructional methods and attitudes related to students with disabilities in higher education. *Exceptionality Education International, 24*(1), 48–64. https://doi.org/10.5206/eei.v25i2.7723

Bolduc, W. (2012). *Unfunded mandate: Does more money mean better special education compliance?* (Doctoral dissertation, Capella University).

Cawthon, S. W., & Cole, E. V. (2010). Postsecondary students who have a learning disability: Student perspectives on accommodations access and obstacles. Journal of Postsecondary Education and Disability, 23(2), 112–128. https://www.ahead.org/publications/jped

Cooc, N. (2019). Do teachers spend less time teaching in classrooms with students with special needs? Trends from international data. *Educational Researcher, 48*(5), 273–286. https://doi-org.lib.pepperdine.edu/10.3102/0013189X19852306

Covey, S. (1992). The Seven Habits of Highly Effective People: Powerful lessons in personal change. Emergency Librarian, 20(1), 62-62.

Daly-Cano, M., Vaccaro, A., & Newman, B. (2015). College student narratives about learning and using self-advocacy skills. *Journal of Postsecondary Education and Disability, 28*(2), 213–227. https://files.eric.ed.gov/fulltext/EJ1074673.pdf

deBettencourt, L. U. (2002). Understanding the Differences between IDEA and Section 504. TEACHING Exceptional Children, 34(3), 16–23. https://doi.org/10.1177/004005990203400302

Dragoo, K. E., & Library of Congress. (2018). The Individuals with Disabilities Education Act (IDEA) funding: A primer. CRS Report R44624, Version 4. Updated. Congressional Research Service. Congressional Research Service. https://fas.org/sgp/crs/misc/R44624.pdf

DSM 5. American Psychiatric Association. (2013). Diagnostic and statistical manual of mental disorders (5th ed.).

DuPaul, G. J., Dahlstrom-Hakki, I., Gormley, M. J., Fu, Q., Pinho, T. D., & Banerjee, M. (2017). College students with ADHD and LD: Effects of support services on academic performance. Learning Disabilities Research & Practice, 32(4), 246–256. https://doi.org/10.1111/ldrp.12143

DuPaul, G. J., Pinho, T. D., Pollack, B. L., Gormley, M. J., & Laracy, S. D. (2017). First-year college students with ADHD and/or LD: Differences in engagement, positive core self-evaluation, school preparation, and college expectations. Journal of Learning Disabilities, 50(3), 238–251. DOI: 10.1177/0022219415617164

Eaton, J. S. (2008). The Higher Education Opportunity Act of 2008: What does it mean and what does it do? https://www.chea.org/higher-education-opportunity-act-2008-what-does-it-mean-and-what-does-it-do

Fishbach, A. (2022). *Get It Done: Surprising Lessons from the Science of Motivation.* Little Brown Spark; New York.

Gitlow, L. (2001). Occupational therapy faculty attitudes toward the inclusion of students with disabilities in their educational programs. The Occupational Therapy Journal of Research, 21(2), 115–131. https://doi.org/10.1177/153944920102100206

Grant, B. (2022). *How to Access College Disability Services and Accommodations.* https://www.bestcolleges.com/blog/how-to-access-college-disability-services/

Grant, P. A., Barger-Anderson, R., Fulcher, P. A., Burkhardt, S., Obiakor, F. E., & Rotatori, A. F. (2004). Impact of the Americans With Disabilities Act on services for persons with learning disabilities. *Current Perspectives on Learning Disabilities, 16,* 183–191. https://doi.org/10.1016/S0270-4013(04)16009-1

Hanson, M. (2022). *College dropout rates.* EducationData.org. https://educationdata.org/college-dropout-rates/

Hegji, A., Fountain, J. H., Collins, B., Kuenzi, J. J., Dortch, C., & Smole, D. P. (2018). HR 4508, the PROSPER Act: Proposed reauthorization of the Higher Education Act. CRS Report R45115, Version 3. Updated. Congressional Research Service.

Hermann, A. M. C. (1977). Sports and the Handicapped: Section 504 of the Rehabilitation Act of 1973 and Curricular, Intramural, Club and Intercollegiate Athletic Programs in Postsecondary Educational Institutions. JC & UL, 5, 143.

Higher Education Opportunity Act Reauthorization. (2008). *Council for exceptional children the voice and vision of special education.* https://www.aucd.org/docs/CEC%20Higher%20Education%20Analysis.pdf

Higher Education Opportunity Act 2008. (2019). https://www2.ed.gov/policy/highered/leg/hea08/index.html

Hong, B. S., & Himmel, J. (2009). Faculty attitudes and perceptions toward college students with disabilities. *College Quarterly*, *12*(3), 678–684. https://files.eric.ed.gov/fulltext/EJ889557.pdf

Hsiao, F., Burgstahler, S., Johnson, T., Nuss, D., & Doherty, M. (2019). Promoting an accessible learning environment for students with disabilities via faculty development (practice brief). *Journal of Postsecondary Education and Disability*, *32*(1), 91–99. https://files.eric.ed.gov/fulltext/EJ1217448.pdf

IES National Center for Education Statistics. (2019). *Students with disabilities at degree-granting postsecondary institutions*. https://nces.ed.gov/pubs2011/2011018.pdf

Jones, S. K. (2015). Teaching students with disabilities: A review of music education research as it relates to the Individuals with Disabilities Education Act. Update: Applications of Research in Music Education, 34(1), 13–23. https://doi.org/10.1177/8755123314548039

LAUSD District Validation Review. Robinson-Neal, A. (2009). Exploring diversity in higher education management: History, trends, and implications for community colleges. *International Electronic Journal for Leadership in Learning*, *13*(4), n4.

Lester, J. N., & Nusbaum, E. A. (2017, September 15). Reclaiming disability in critical qualitative research: Introduction to the special issue. Qualitative Inquiry, 24(1), 3–7. https://doi.org/10.1177/1077800417727761

Leuchovius, D. (2003). ADA Q&A…the ADA, section 504 & postsecondary education. *Pacer Center Action Information Sheets*.

Leyser, Y., Greenberger, L., Sharoni, V., & Vogel, G. (2011). Students with disabilities in teacher education: Changes in faculty attitudes toward accommodations over ten years. *International Journal of Special Education, 26*(1), 162–174. https://files.eric.ed.gov/fulltext/EJ921202.pdf

Lombardi, A., McGuire, J. M., & Tarconish, E. (2018). Promoting inclusive teaching among college faculty: A framework for disability service providers (practice brief). *Journal of Postsecondary Education and Disability, 31*(4), 397–413. https://files.eric.ed.gov/fulltext/EJ1214261.pdf

Lombardi, A., Murray, C., & Dallas, B. (2013). University faculty attitudes toward disability and inclusive instruction: Comparing two institutions. *Journal of Postsecondary Education and Disability, 26*(3), 221–232. https://files.eric.ed.gov/fulltext/EJ1026882.pdf

Lombardi, A. R., Murray, C., & Gerdes, H. (2011). College faculty and inclusive instruction: Self-reported attitudes and actions pertaining to universal design. *Journal of Diversity in Higher Education, 4*(4), 250–261. DOI: 10.1037/a0024961

Madaus, J. W., Kowitt, J. S., & Lalor, A. R. (2012). The Higher Education Opportunity Act: Impact on students with disabilities. Rehabilitation Research, Policy & Education, 26(1). DOI: 10.1891/216866512805000893

Madaus, J. W., & Shaw, S. F. (2004). Section 504: Differences in the regulations for secondary and postsecondary education. Intervention in School and Clinic, 40(2), 81–87. https://doi.org/10.1177/10534512040400020301

Mathis, W. J., & Trujillo, T. M. (2016). Lessons from NCLB for the Every Student Succeeds Act. *National Education Policy Center*. https://files.eric.ed.gov/fulltext/ED574684.pdf

Mongiovi, K. A. (2012). *Faculty provisions of accommodations for students with disabilities in higher education: An analysis of community college faculty in the traditional, hybrid, and online mathematics course teaching environments.* Publication No. 3569632. [University of Florida]. Proquest Dissertations and Theses Database.

Murray, C., Lombardi, A., Wren, C. T., & Keys, C. (2009). Associations between prior disability-focused training and disability-related attitudes and perceptions among university faculty. Learning Disability Quarterly, 32(2), 87–100. DOI: 10.2307/27740359

Murray, C., Wren, C. T., & Keys, C. (2008). University faculty perceptions of students with learning disabilities: Correlates and group differences. Learning Disability Quarterly, 31(3), 95–113. https://doi.org/10.2307/25474642

National Center for Education Statistics. (2020). https://nces.ed.gov/surveys/peqis/publications/1999046/index.asp?sectionID=3

Newman, L. A., & Madaus, J. W. (2015). Reported accommodations and supports provided to secondary and postsecondary students with disabilities: National perspective. *Career Development and Transition for Exceptional Individuals, 38*(3), 173–181. https://doi.org/10.1177/2165143413518235

Newman, L. A., Madaus, J. W., & Javitz, H. S. (2016). Effect of transition planning on postsecondary support receipt by students with disabilities. *Exceptional Children, 82*(4), 497–514. https://doi.org/10.1177/0014402915615884

Newman, L. A., Madaus, J. W., Lalor, A. R., & Javitz, H. S. (2019). Support receipt: Effect on postsecondary success of students with learning disabilities. *Career Development and Transition for Exceptional Individuals, 42*(1), 6–16. https://doi.org/10.1177/2165143418811288

Olkin, R. (2002). Could you hold the door for me? Including disability in diversity. Cultural Diversity and Ethnic Minority Psychology, 8(2), 130–137. https://doi.org/10.1037/1099-9809.8.2.130

Prince, A. M., Katsiyannis, A., & Farmer, J. (2013). Postsecondary transition under IDEA 2004: A legal update. *Intervention in School and Clinic, 48*(5), 286–293. https://doi.org/10.1177/1053451212472233

Rao, S. (2004). Faculty attitudes and students with disabilities in higher education: A literature review. *College Student Journal, 38*(2), 191–199.

Rao, S., & Gartin, B. C. (2003). Attitudes of university faculty toward accommodations to students with disabilities. *Journal for Vocational Special Needs Education, 25*, 47–54.

Schreifels, J. M. (2013). *Self-advocacy from the perspective of young adults with specific learning disabilities during the transition process* (Doctoral dissertation, Walden University).

Sinek, S. (2009). *Start with why: How great leaders inspire everyone to take action.* Penguin.

Smith, T. E. (2005). IDEA 2004: Another round in the reauthorization process. Remedial and Special Education, 26(6), 314–319. https://doi.org/10.1177/07419325050260060101

Sniatecki, J. L., Perry, H. B., & Snell, L. H. (2015). Faculty attitudes and knowledge regarding college students with disabilities. *Journal of Postsecondary Education and Disability, 28*(3), 259–275. https://files.eric.ed.gov/fulltext/EJ1083837.pdf

Tinto, V. (1988). Stages of student departure: Reflections on the longitudinal character of student leaving. The Journal of Higher Education, 59(4), 438–455. https://doi.org/10.2307/1981920

Tonsager, L., & Skeath, C. W. (2017). Ask and you might not receive: How FERPA's disclosure provisions can affect educational research. *Journal of Student Financial Aid, 47*(3), 6. 87–96.
https://files.eric.ed.gov/fulltext/EJ1160073.pdf

U.S. Department of Education. (2020). *Higher Education Opportunity Act-2008.*
https://www2.ed.gov/policy/highered/leg/hea08/index.html

U.S. Department of Education. (2020). *Welcome to OSEP. OSERS Office of Special Education Programs.*
https://www2.ed.gov/about/offices/list/osers/osep/index.html

U.S. Department of Education. Office for Civil Rights. (2019). *Students with disabilities: Preparing for postsecondary education.*
https://www2.ed.gov/about/offices/list/ocr/transition.html

U.S. Department of Education, Office for Civil Rights. (2020). *Protecting students with disabilities.*
https://www2.ed.gov/about/offices/list/ocr/504faq.html

U.S. Department of Education, National Center for Education Statistics. (2019). *Digest of Education Statistics, 2018* (2020-009), Chapter 3.

Vogel, S. A., Leyser, Y., Wyland, S., & Brulle, A. (1999). Students with learning disabilities in higher education: Faculty attitude and practices. *Learning Disabilities Research & Practice, 14*(3), 173–186. https://web-b-ebscohost-com.lib.pepperdine.edu/ehost/pdfviewer/pdfviewer?vid=12&sid=414ba448-63b5-4d8b-9b56-538eb910b768%40pdc-v-sessmgr05

West, E. A., Novak, D., & Mueller, C. (2016). Inclusive instructional practices used and their perceived importance by instructors. *Journal of Postsecondary Education and Disability, 29*(4), 363–374. https://files.eric.ed.gov/fulltext/EJ1133764.pdf

West Chester University. (2018). *Differences between HS and college for students with disabilities.* https://www.wcupa.edu/viceProvost/ussss/ossd/documents/RevisedADAhandbook.pdf

Wilkinson, T., & Reinhardt, R. (2015). Technology in counselor education: HIPAA and HITECH as best practice. *Professional Counselor, 5*(3), 407–418. https://files.eric.ed.gov/fulltext/EJ1069426.pdf

APPENDICES

Appendix 1.

Definitions of Special Education Terms and Acronyms (Baker, 2021)

Americans with Disabilities Act (ADA): prohibits discrimination on the basis of disability in employment, state and local government, public accommodations, commercial facilities, transportation, and telecommunications. It also applies to the United States Congress.

Accessibility: When a person **with** a disability is afforded the opportunity to acquire the same information, engage in the same interactions, and enjoy the same services as a person without a disability in an equally integrated and equally effective manner, with substantially equivalent ease of use. It guarantees SWDs are provided with curriculum materials in necessary formats and technologies with appropriate features in a timely manner and at the same time as students without disabilities.

Accommodations: Changes that allow a person with a disability to participate fully in an activity. Examples may include extended time, different test format, and alterations to a classroom. The Case Study Committee (CSC) determines what accommodations are required and once an accommodation is on an Individualized Education Plan (IEP), they are not optional. Accommodations are reviewed annually and will need to be modified on an annual basis. An *accommodation* changes how a student learns the material. A *modification* changes what a student is taught or expected to learn.

Attention Deficit Hyperactivity Disorder (ADHD): A disorder that causes children to struggle with paying attention, being extremely active, and acting impulsively.

Accessibility Services/Disability Services (DS): Provides coordination of support services and accommodations for all qualified SWDs. Through collaboration and support of the entire campus community, the Accessibility Services Office ensures that all individuals have access to college life at its fullest. Services and accommodations are determined individually based on disability documentation.

Assistive technology: Any item, piece of equipment, or product system, whether acquired commercially off the shelf, modified, or customized, that is used to increase, maintain, or improve functional capabilities of a child with a disability.

Confidentiality: The IDEA requires procedures to provide a Free Appropriate Public Education (FAPE) for all children with disabilities and are safeguards prohibiting the disclosure of any personally identifiable information. Clear guidelines have been set forth for public schools when collecting, storing, releasing, or destroying personally identifiable information on students.

Culture: The shared assumptions of individuals participating in an organization, identified through stories, special language, norms, institutional ideology, and attitudes that emerge from the individual or organizational behavior, and organizational web bound by a structure.

Every Student Succeeds Act (ESSA): signed into law in 2015 and replaced No Child Left Behind.

Free Appropriate Public Education (FAPE): An educational right of children with disabilities guaranteed by the IDEA. FAPE is defined as an educational program that is individualized to a specific child, designed to meet that child's unique needs, provides access to the general curriculum, meets the grade-level standards established by the school system, and from which the child receives educational benefit.

Health Insurance Portability Accountability Act (HIPAA): HIPAA of 1996 is United States legislation that provides data privacy and security provisions for safeguarding medical information.

Individuals with Disabilities Education Act (IDEA): The original legislation was written in 1975, guaranteeing SWDs a FAPE and the right to be educated with their nondisabled peers. Congress has reauthorized this federal law. The most recent revision occurred in 2004.

Individual Education Plan (IEP): Education plan provided to all students with a disability that have been found eligible for special education services and it is a written plan that specifies the individual educational needs of the student and what special education and related services are necessary to meet the student's unique instructional needs.

Individualized Transition Plan: This plan starts at age sixteen and includes a statement about transition out of public education. This plan consists of goals that address areas of post-school activities, postsecondary education, employment, community experiences, and daily living skills. The plan includes services needed to achieve these goals.

Intellectual Disabilities: A disability characterized by significant limitations both in intellectual functioning and in adaptive behavior as expressed in conceptual, social, and practical adaptive skills; deficit in cognitive functioning prior to the acquisition of skills through learning. The intensity of the deficit is such that it interferes in a significant way with individual normal functioning as expressed in limitations in activities and restriction in participation (disabilities).

Least Restrictive Environment: The placement of a special needs student in a manner promoting the maximum possible interaction with the general school population. Placement options are offered on a continuum, including regular classroom with no support services, regular classroom with support services, designated instruction services, special day classes, and private special education programs.

Modification: An adjustment to an assignment or a test that changes the standard or what the test or assignment is supposed to measure.

No Child Left Behind (NCLB): Passed in 2001 to improve student achievement, reform educational programs ensure that all children have the fair, equal opportunity to obtain a high-quality education, and reach, at a minimum, proficiency on challenging state academic achievement standards.

Specific Learning Disability: A condition giving rise to difficulties in acquiring knowledge and skills to the level expected of those of the same age, especially when not associated with a physical handicap.

Special Education Advocates or IEP Advocates: These help parents write appropriate IEPs and attain special education services for their child with a disability from their public-school system.

Specially Designed Instruction (SDI): As detailed in IDEA legislation, includes structured collaboration and delineated roles for each teacher, and emphasis on one-on-one instruction between students and special education teachers.

SOP: Documents a child's academic achievement and functional performance including recommendations on how to assist the child in meeting the child's postsecondary goals. It is provided to a child whose eligibility for special education services has terminated "due to graduation from secondary school with a regular diploma, or due to exceeding the age eligibility for a free appropriate public education under State law" (Individuals with Disabilities Education Act of 2004 [IDEA].

Transition Services: These identify each student's long-range goals relative to postsecondary education (including their strengths, preferences, and interests) vocational education, integrated employment continuing adult education, adult services an independent living.

Universal Design of Learning (UDL): A set of principles for designing curriculum that provides all individuals with equal opportunities to learn. UDL is designed to serve all learners, regardless of ability, disability, age, gender, or cultural and linguistic background. UDL provides a blueprint for designing goals, methods, materials, and assessments to reach all students, including those with diverse needs.

ABOUT THE AUTHOR

Toby Tomlinson Baker has earned her Ph.D. from Pepperdine University and is a professor at California State University-Los Angeles. She continues to serve students and families of the Los Angeles Unified School District. She has thirteen years of experience as a special educator with a deep understanding of disabilities through the special circumstance of having a learning disability and ADHD herself.

In 2018, Dr. Baker was awarded Children and Adults with ADHD-CHADD's *Educator of the Year*. She has been recognized as a Top Performing Educator by LAUSD's superintendent and was awarded the Harrison Sylvester Award in 2020 for her research by the Learning Disability Association of America (LDA). In 2021, Dr. Baker was awarded the Top Education Policy Writer for the award-winning magazine *Exceptional Needs Today!* and was on the cover of the July edition with her story.

Today, Dr. Baker is a tireless advocate and global speaker who champions perseverance and determination as instrumental in the academic success for students with disabilities. She has written numerous Opinion Editorials and presented policy briefs to the Department of Education, National Organization on Disability, members of Congress, and the White House. She continues to share the story of her educational journey and her strategies for success during college in her book, *The Traveling IEP*.

Toby Tomlinson Baker, Ph.D.
tobytomlinsonbaker@gmail.com
https://tobytomlinsonbaker.net
Research: accommodations, ADHD, advocacy, best practices, disabilities, faculty, policy

NOTES

[1] IDEA Specially Designed Instruction is written explicitly in the public law, the Individuals with Disabilities Act. (Prince, A. M., Katsiyannis, A., & Farmer, J. (2013). Postsecondary transition under IDEA 2004: A legal update. *Intervention in School and Clinic, 48*(5), 286–293. P 4.

The ARC, (2022). *6 Principals of the IEP.* © The Arc - Jefferson, Clear Creek & Gilpin Counties 2022.
https://www.arcjc.org/gethelp/classestraining/idea/ideaiep.html

[2] 72% of all students with disabilities have departed or dropped out of postsecondary academic settings (college and universities), including online and distance learning. (IES National Center for Education Statistics. 2019). p. 7.

[3] The ARC, (2022). *6 Principals of the IEP.* © The Arc - Jefferson, Clear Creek & Gilpin
Counties 2022.
https://www.arcjc.org/gethelp/classestraining/idea/ideaiep.html

[4] Rehabilitation Act. Leuchovius, D. (2003). ADA Q&A…the ADA, section 504 & postsecondary education. *Pacer Center Action Information Sheets.* p. 8.

[5] IDEA Specially Designed Instruction is written explicitly in the public law, the Individuals with Disabilities Act. (Prince, A. M., Katsiyannis, A., & Farmer, J. (2013). Postsecondary transition under IDEA 2004: A legal update. *Intervention in School and Clinic, 48*(5), 286–293. P 8.

[6] Attention deficit hyperactivity disorder. DuPaul, G. J., Dahlstrom-Hakki, I., Gormley, M. J., Fu, Q., Pinho, T. D., & Banerjee, M. (2017). College students with ADHD and LD: Effects of support services on academic performance. Learning Disabilities Research & Practice, 32(4), 246–256. https://doi.org/10.1111/ldrp.12143 p. 8.

[7] Rehabilitation Act. Leuchovius, D. (2003). ADA Q&A…the ADA, section 504 & postsecondary education. *Pacer Center Action Information Sheets.* p. 9.

[8] Rehabilitation Act. Leuchovius, D. (2003). ADA Q&A…the ADA, section 504 & postsecondary education. *Pacer Center Action Information Sheets.* p. 10.

[9] ADA. Grant, P. A., Barger-Anderson, R., Fulcher, P. A., et. al., (2004). Impact of the Americans with Disabilities Act on services for persons with learning disabilities. *Current Perspectives on Learning Disabilities, 16*, 183–191. https://doi.org/10.1016/S0270-4013(04)16009-1 p. 11.

[10] Self-efficacy. Bandura, A. (1997). *Self-efficacy: The exercise of control*. WH Freeman. p. 11.

[11] IES National Center for Education Statistics. (2019). *Students with disabilities at degree-granting postsecondary institutions.* https://nces.ed.gov/pubs2011/2011018.pdf p.12.

[12] Olkin, R. (2002). *Could you hold the door for me? Including disability in diversity.* Cultural Diversity and Ethnic Minority Psychology, 8(2), 130–137. https://doi.org/10.1037/1099-9809.8.2.130 p. 13.

[13] Specially Designed Instruction is written explicitly in the public law, the Individuals with Disabilities Act. (Prince, A. M., Katsiyannis, A., & Farmer, J. (2013). Postsecondary transition under IDEA 2004: A legal update. *Intervention in School and Clinic, 48*(5), 286–293. p.15.

[14] Specially Designed Instruction is written explicitly in the public law, the Individuals with Disabilities Act. (Prince, A. M., Katsiyannis, A., & Farmer, J. (2013). Postsecondary transition under IDEA 2004: A legal update. *Intervention in School and Clinic, 48*(5), 286–293. Pp. 15-16.

[15] Specially Designed Instruction as detailed in the IDEA, places a heavy emphasis on one-on-one instruction between SWDs and faculty. Madaus, J. W., & Shaw, S. F. (2004). Section 504: Differences in the regulations for secondary and postsecondary education. Intervention in School and Clinic, 40(2), 81–87. https://doi.org/10.1177/10534512040400020301 p.16.

[16] SAMUELS, CHRISTINA (2014). LANDMARK SPECIAL ED. CASE CONFIRMING 'ZERO REJECT' RULE MARKS 25 YEARS. https://www.edweek.org/policy-politics/landmark-special-ed-case-confirming-zero-reject-rule-marks-25-years/2014/12

[17] High school graduates and enrollment in postsecondary settings ensued. Hanson, M. (2022). *College dropout rates.* EducationData.org. https://educationdata.org/college-dropout-rates/ p. 17.

[18] The ASHA leader, (2018, February 1). Graduation Rate for U.S. Students With Disabilities Hits 65.5 Percent. Vol. 23, Issue 2. https://doi.org/10.1044/leader.NIB4.23022018.16 p.18.

[19] Throughout each decade, previous legislation has been passed to protect SWDs such as Section 504 Rehabilitation Act. (Grant, P. A., Barger-Anderson, R., Fulcher, P. A., Burkhardt, S., Obiakor, F. E., & Rotatori, A. F. (2004). Impact of the Americans with Disabilities Act on services for persons with learning disabilities. *Current Perspectives on Learning Disabilities, 16*, 183–191. https://doi.org/10.1016/S0270-4013(04)16009-1 p. 18.

[20] Gitlow, L. (2001). Occupational therapy faculty attitudes toward the inclusion of students with disabilities in their educational programs. The Occupational Therapy Journal of Research, 21(2), 115–131. https://doi.org/10.1177/153944920102100206 p. 19.

[21] Hegji, A., Fountain, J. H., Collins, B., Kuenzi, J. J., Dortch, C., & Smole, D. P. (2018). HR 4508, the PROSPER Act: Proposed reauthorization of the Higher Education Act. CRS Report R45115, Version 3. Updated. Congressional Research Service. p.20.

[22] ADA-The focus is on discrimination not academic accommodations. Grant, P. A., Barger-Anderson, R., Fulcher, P. A., Burkhardt, S., Obiakor, F. E., & Rotatori, A. F. (2004). Impact of the Americans With Disabilities Act on services for persons with learning disabilities. *Current Perspectives on Learning Disabilities, 16*, 183–191. https://doi.org/10.1016/S0270-4013(04)16009-1 p. 21.

[23] **U.S. DEPARTMENT OF EDUCATION (2022). 2021 ANNUAL REPORT TO CONGRESS ON THE INDIVIDUALS WITH DISABILITIES EDUCATION ACT (IDEA).HTTPS://SITES.ED.GOV/IDEA/2021-INDIVIDUALS-WITH-DISABILITIES-EDUCATION-ACT-ANNUAL-REPORT-TO-CONGRESS/**

[24] HEOA Newman, L. A., & Madaus, J. W. (2015). Reported accommodations and supports provided to secondary and postsecondary students with disabilities: National perspective. *Career Development and Transition for Exceptional Individuals, 38*(3), 173–181. https://doi.org/10.1177/2165143413518235 p. 22.

[25] Mathis, W. J., & Trujillo, T. M. (2016). Lessons from NCLB for the Every Student Succeeds Act. *National Education Policy Center.* https://files.eric.ed.gov/fulltext/ED574684.pdf p. 22.

[26] Necessary services and accommodations in higher education. Adreon, D., & Durocher, J. S. (2007). Evaluating the college transition needs of individuals with high-functioning autism spectrum disorders. *Intervention in School and Clinic, 42*(5), 271–279. https://doi.org/10.1177/10534512070420050201https://doi.org/10.1177/10534512070420050201 p. 23.

[27] Bolduc, W. (2012). *Unfunded mandate: Does more money mean better special education compliance?* (Doctoral dissertation, Capella University). p. 24.

[28] Section 504. U.S. Department of Education. (2020a). *Welcome to OSEP. OSERS Office of Special Education Programs.* https://www2.ed.gov/about/offices/list/osers/osep/index.html

[29] Even though SWDs are guaranteed rights for coverage of a disability, they may not receive the same and necessary services and accommodations. Adreon, D., & Durocher, J. S. (2007). Evaluating the college transition needs of individuals with high-functioning autism spectrum disorders. *Intervention in School and Clinic, 42*(5), 271–279. https://doi.org/10.1177/10534512070420050201https://doi.org/10.1177/10534512070420050201 p. 24.

[30] Not mandated to provide accommodations. DuPaul, G. J., Dahlstrom-Hakki, I., Gormley, M. J., Fu, Q., Pinho, T. D., & Banerjee, M. (2017). College students with ADHD and LD: Effects of support services on academic performance. Learning Disabilities Research & Practice, 32(4), 246–256. https://doi.org/10.1111/ldrp.12143 p. 27

[31] Postsecondary institutions are required to *provide appropriate academic adjustments* to ensure that the institution does not discriminate based on disability. Bays, D. A. (2001). *Supervision of special education instruction in rural public-school districts: A grounded theory* [Doctoral dissertation, Virginia Tech]. p. 29.

[32] U.S. Department of Education, Office for Civil Rights. (2020). *Protecting students with disabilities.* https://www2.ed.gov/about/offices/list/ocr/504faq.html p. 29.

[33] IDEA coverage. deBettencourt, L. U. (2002). Understanding the Differences between IDEA and Section 504. TEACHING Exceptional Children, 34(3), 16–23. https://doi.org/10.1177/004005990203400302 p. 30.

[34] Bailey, A. B., & Smith, S. W. (2000). Current topics in review: Providing effective coping

strategies and supports for families with children with disabilities. *Intervention in School and Clinic*, 35(5), 294-296. p. 34. https://journals.sagepub.com/doi/pdf/10.1177/105345120003500507

[35] Cawthon, S. W., & Cole, E. V. (2010). Postsecondary students who have a learning disability: Student perspectives on accommodations access and obstacles. Journal of Postsecondary Education and Disability, 23(2), 112-128. https://www.ahead.org/publications/jped p. 34.

[36] West Chester University. (2018). *Differences between HS and college for students with disabilities.* https://www.wcupa.edu/viceProvost/ussss/ossd/documents/RevisedADAhandbook.pdf p. 34.

[37] Leyser, Y., Greenberger, L., Sharoni, V., & Vogel, G. (2011). Students with disabilities in teacher education: Changes in faculty attitudes toward accommodations over ten years. *International Journal of Special Education*, 26(1), 162-174. p. 33. https://files.eric.ed.gov/fulltext/EJ921202.pdf

[38] HIPAA. Wilkinson, T., & Reinhardt, R. (2015). Technology in counselor education: HIPAA and HITECH as best practice. *Professional Counselor,* 5(3), 407-418. https://files.eric.ed.gov/fulltext/EJ1069426.pdf p. 35.

[39] FERPA. Tonsager, L., & Skeath, C. W. (2017). Ask and you might not receive: How FERPA's disclosure provisions can affect educational research. *Journal of Student Financial Aid,* 47(3), 6. 87-96. https://files.eric.ed.gov/fulltext/EJ1160073.pdf p. 35.

[40] Baker, T. T. (2021). *Support for students with disabilities: How awareness and accommodations differ across faculty members within the postsecondary context* (Order No. 28539983). Available from ProQuest Dissertations & Theses Global. (2543424985). p. 42.

[41] Bays, D. A. (2001). *Supervision of special education instruction in rural public-school districts: A grounded theory* [Doctoral dissertation, Virginia Tech]. p. 38.

[42] Lombardi, A., Murray, C., & Dallas, B. (2013). University faculty attitudes toward disability and inclusive instruction: Comparing two institutions. *Journal of Postsecondary Education and Disability*, 26(3), 221–232. https://files.eric.ed.gov/fulltext/EJ1026882.pdf p. 39.

[43] Baker, T. T. (2021). *Support for students with disabilities: How awareness and accommodations differ across faculty members within the postsecondary context* (Order No. 28539983). Available from ProQuest Dissertations & Theses Global. (2543424985). p. 40.

[44] Baker, T. T. (2021). *Support for students with disabilities: How awareness and accommodations differ across faculty members within the postsecondary context* (Order No. 28539983). Available from ProQuest Dissertations & Theses Global. (2543424985). p. 40.

[45] Baker, T. T. (2021). *Support for students with disabilities: How awareness and accommodations differ across faculty members within the postsecondary context* (Order No. 28539983). Available from ProQuest Dissertations & Theses Global. (2543424985). p. 41.

[46] West, E. A., Novak, D., & Mueller, C. (2016). Inclusive instructional practices used and their perceived importance by instructors. *Journal of Postsecondary Education and Disability, 29*(4), 363–374. https://files.eric.ed.gov/fulltext/EJ1133764.pdf p. 50.

[47] Vogel, S. A., Leyser, Y., Wyland, S., & Brulle, A. (1999). Students with learning disabilities in higher education: Faculty attitude and practices. *Learning Disabilities Research & Practice, 14*(3), 173–186. p. 46.https://web-b-ebscohost-com.lib.pepperdine.edu/ehost/pdfviewer/pdfviewer?vid=12&sid=414ba448-63b5-4d8b-9b56-538eb910b768%40pdc-v-sessmgr05 p. 53.

[48] Daly-Cano, M., Vaccaro, A., & Newman, B. (2015). College student narratives about learning and using self-advocacy skills. *Journal of Postsecondary Education and Disability, 28*(2), 213–227. https://files.eric.ed.gov/fulltext/EJ1074673.pdf p. 54.

[49] Baker, T. T. (2021). Support for students with disabilities: How awareness and accommodations differ across faculty members within the postsecondary context (Order No. 28539983). Available from ProQuest Dissertations & Theses Global. (2543424985). p. 55.

[50] Leyser, Y., Greenberger, L., Sharoni, V., & Vogel, G. (2011). Students with disabilities in teacher education: Changes in faculty attitudes toward accommodations over ten years. *International Journal of Special Education, 26*(1), 162–174. https://files.eric.ed.gov/fulltext/EJ921202.pdf p. 56.

[51] Baker, T. T. (2021). Support for students with disabilities: How awareness and accommodations differ across faculty members within the postsecondary context (Order No. 28539983). Available from ProQuest Dissertations & Theses Global. (2543424985). p. 56.

[52] Black, R. D., Weinberg, L. A., & Brodwin, M. G. (2014). Universal design for instruction and learning: A pilot study of faculty instructional methods and attitudes related to students with disabilities in higher education. *Exceptionality Education International, 24*(1), 48–64. https://doi.org/10.5206/eei.v25i2.7723 p. 56.

[53] Rao, S., & Gartin, B. C. (2003). Attitudes of university faculty toward accommodations to students with disabilities. *Journal for Vocational Special Needs Education, 25*, 47–54. p. 57.

[54] Madaus, J. W., Kowitt, J. S., & Lalor, A. R. (2012). The Higher Education Opportunity Act: Impact on students with disabilities. Rehabilitation Research, Policy & Education, 26(1). doi:10.1891/216866512805000893 p. 57.

[55] DSM 5. American Psychiatric Association. (2013). Diagnostic and statistical manual of mental disorders (5th ed.). https://doi.org/10.1176/appi.books.9780890425596 p. 57.

[56] Sniatecki, J. L., Perry, H. B., & Snell, L. H. (2015). Faculty attitudes and knowledge regarding college students with disabilities. *Journal of Postsecondary Education and Disability*, 28(3), 259–275. https://files.eric.ed.gov/fulltext/EJ1083837.pdf p. 57.

[57] Vogel, S. A., Leyser, Y., Wyland, S., & Brulle, A. (1999). Students with learning disabilities in higher education: Faculty attitude and practices. *Learning Disabilities Research & Practice*, 14(3), 173–186. https://web-b-ebscohost-com.lib.pepperdine.edu/ehost/pdfviewer/pdfviewer?vid=12&sid=414ba448-63b5-4d8b-9b56-538eb910b768%40pdc-v-sessmgr05 p. 58.

[58] West, E. A., Novak, D., & Mueller, C. (2016). Inclusive instructional practices used and their perceived importance by instructors. *Journal of Postsecondary Education and Disability*, 29(4), 363–374. https://files.eric.ed.gov/fulltext/EJ1133764.pdf p. 59.

[59] **GRANT, B. (2022). HOW TO ACCESS COLLEGE DISABILITY SERVICES AND ACCOMMODATIONS.** https://www.bestcolleges.com/blog/how-to-access-college-disability-services/

[60] Murray, C., Wren, C. T., & Keys, C. (2008). University faculty perceptions of students with learning disabilities: Correlates and group differences. Learning Disability Quarterly, 31(3), 95–113. https://doi.org/10.2307/25474642 p. 59.

[61] Jones, S. K. (2015). Teaching students with disabilities: A review of music education research as it relates to the Individuals with Disabilities Education Act. Update: Applications of Research in Music Education, 34(1), 13–23. https://doi.org/10.1177/8755123314548039 p. 61.

[62] Jones, S. K. (2015). Teaching students with disabilities: A review of music education research as it relates to the Individuals with Disabilities Education Act. Update: Applications of Research in Music Education, 34(1), 13–23. https://doi.org/10.1177/8755123314548039 p. 61.

[63] Lombardi, A. R., Murray, C., & Gerdes, H. (2011). College faculty and inclusive instruction: Self-reported attitudes and actions pertaining to universal design. *Journal of Diversity in Higher Education, 4*(4), 250–261. DOI: 10.1037/a0024961 p. 62.

[64] DuPaul, G. J., Pinho, T. D., Pollack, B. L., Gormley, M. J., & Laracy, S. D. (2017). First-year college students with ADHD and/or LD: Differences in engagement, positive core self-evaluation, school preparation, and college expectations. Journal of Learning Disabilities, 50(3), 238–251. DOI: 10.1177/0022219415617164 p. 62.

[65] DuPaul, G. J., Pinho, T. D., Pollack, B. L., Gormley, M. J., & Laracy, S. D. (2017). First-year college students with ADHD and/or LD: Differences in engagement, positive core self-evaluation, school preparation, and college expectations. Journal of Learning Disabilities, 50(3), 238–251. DOI: 10.1177/0022219415617164 p. 64.

[66] Covey, S. (1992). *The Seven Habits of Highly Effective People: Powerful Lessons in Personal Change.* Emergency Librarian, 20(1), 62-62. p. 64.

[67] Sinek, S. (2009). *Start with Why: How Great Leaders Inspire Everyone to Take Action.* Penguin. p. 64.

[68] Mongiovi, K. A. (2012). *Faculty provisions of accommodations for students with disabilities in higher education: An analysis of community college faculty in the traditional, hybrid, and online mathematics course teaching environments.* Publication No. 3569632. [University of Florida]. Proquest Dissertations and Theses Database. p. 66.

[69] Faculty respondents also expressed strong interest in professional development opportunities related to SWDs. Sniatecki, J. L., Perry, H. B., & Snell, L. H. (2015). Faculty attitudes and knowledge regarding college students with disabilities. *Journal of Postsecondary Education and Disability, 28*(3), 259–275. https://files.eric.ed.gov/fulltext/EJ1083837.pdf p. 66.

[70] Because faculty have had good experiences with SWDs, they have a positive perception about them. As a result of this positivity, professors are willing and can accommodate SWDs. Sniatecki, J. L., Perry, H. B., & Snell, L. H. (2015). Faculty attitudes and knowledge regarding college students with disabilities. *Journal of Postsecondary Education and Disability*, 28(3), 259–275. https://files.eric.ed.gov/fulltext/EJ1083837.pdf p. 67.

[71] Fishbach, A. (2022). *Get It Done: Surprising Lessons from the Science of Motivation.* Little Brown Spark; New York. p. 67.

[72] Michalski, J. H., Cunningham, T., & Henry, J. (2017). The diversity challenge for higher education in Canada: The prospects and challenges of increased access and student success. *Humboldt Journal of Social Relations*, 39, 66-89. p. 68.

[73] Cooc, N. (2019). Do teachers spend less time teaching in classrooms with students with special needs? Trends from international data. *Educational Researcher, 48*(5), 273–286. p. 69.

[74] LAUSD District Validation Review. Robinson-Neal, A. (2009). Exploring diversity in higher education management: History, trends, and implications for community colleges. *International Electronic Journal for Leadership in Learning*, 13(4), n4. p. 69.

[75] Vogel, S. A., Leyser, Y., Wyland, S., & Brulle, A. (1999). Students with learning disabilities in higher education: Faculty attitude and practices. *Learning Disabilities Research & Practice, 14*(3), 173–186. p. 71.

[76] Higher Education Opportunity Act 2008. (2019). https://www2.ed.gov/policy/highered/leg/hea08/index.html p. 73.

[77] Rehabilitation Act. Hermann, A. M. C. (1977). Sports and the Handicapped: Section 504 of the Rehabilitation Act of 1973 and Curricular, Intramural, Club and Intercollegiate Athletic Programs in Postsecondary Educational Institutions. JC & UL, 5, 143. p. 73.

[78] Higher Education Opportunity Act Reauthorization. (2008). *Council for exceptional children the voice and vision of special education.* https://www.aucd.org/docs/CEC%20Higher%20Education%20Analysis.pdf p. 73.

[79] Diana DeGette introduced the RISE Act. H.R.869 – 117th Congress (2021-2022): RISE Act of 2021. (2021, February 5). https://www.congress.gov/bill/117th-congress/house-bill/869/text p. 74.

[80] Bob Casey Jr. introduced the RISE Act. H.R.869 – 117th Congress (2021-2022): RISE Act of 2021. (2021, July 29). https://www.congress.gov/bill/117th-congress/senate-bill/2550/text p. 75.

[81] Baker, T. T. (2021 August 6). Senator Casey is Right: Congress Needs to Help College Students with Disabilities. *PennLive; Harrisburg Patriot News.* https://www.pennlive.com/opinion/2021/08/sen-casey-is-right-congress-needs-to-help-college-students-with-disabilities-opinion.html p. 75.

[82] Mark DeSaulnier introduced Mental Health Matters Act. H.R.7780 – 117th Congress (2021-2022): RISE Act of 2021. (2022 May 16). https://www.govinfo.gov/app/details/BILLS-117hr7780ih p. 78.

[83] Baker, T. T. (2018). *The Concealed Population of Students with Learning Disabilities and the Quiet Advocacy of Families in Southeast Asia.* Journal of Global Leadership. Pepperdine University, December 2018. p. 81.

[84] Lester, J. N., & Nusbaum, E. A. (2017, September 15). Reclaiming disability in critical qualitative research: Introduction to the special issue. Qualitative Inquiry, 24(1), 3–7. https://doi.org/10.1177/1077800417727761 p. 83.

Made in the USA
Las Vegas, NV
31 August 2023